The Beggar's Opera

The Beggar's Opera

VÁCLAV HAVEL

TRANSLATED FROM THE CZECH BY
PAUL WILSON

INTRODUCTION BY
PETER STEINER

CORNELL UNIVERSITY PRESS
Ithaca and London

First published 2001 by Cornell University Press

Printed in the United States of America

Library of Congress Cataloging-in-Publication Data

Havel, Václav
  [Žebracká opera. English]
  The beggar's opera / by Vaclav Havel ; translated from the Czech by Paul Wilson ;
introduction by Peter Steiner.
     p.   cm.
  Based on: The Beggar's opera by John Gay.
  ISBN 0-8014-3833-0 (cloth : alk. paper)
  I. Wilson, Paul R. (Paul Robert), 1941-   . II. Gay, John,
1685-1732. Beggar's opera. III. Title.
  PG5039.18.A9 Z313 2001
  891.8'6254—dc21

                                                                00-011737

Cornell University Press strives to use environmentally responsible suppliers and
materials to the fullest extent possible in the publishing of its books. Such materials
include vegetable-based, low-VOC inks and acid-free papers that are recycled, totally
chlorine-free, or partly composed of nonwood fibers. Books that bear the logo of the
FSC (Forest Stewardship Council) use paper taken from forests that have been
inspected and certified as meeting the highest standards for environmental and social
responsibility. For further information, visit our website at
www.cornellpress.cornell.edu.

Cloth printing   10 9 8 7 6 5 4 3 2 1

Contents

Illustrations

Note: All photographs are by Bohdan Holomíček. They were taken at the time of the premiere performance of *The Beggar's Opera* in the House of Culture, Horní Počernice, Czechoslovakia, on 1 November 1975.

Introduction

Peter Steiner

LOCKIT. Lions, Wolves, and Vultures don't live together in Herds, Droves or Flocks. Of all Animals of Prey, Man is the sociable one.
—John Gay, *The Beggar's Opera*

Lockit's wry observation likening man to predatory beasts aptly fits the altogether misanthropic view of the human race that pervades John Gay's play. But, at the same time, this metaphor also suggests its own limits. Man is similar to lions, wolves, or vultures, Lockit is saying, because his behavior is driven by the same killer instinct. Yet, unlike them, he is also a social being. Presented in this way, human existence is a paradox, a case of bipolar disorder: a never ending oscillation between the extremes of individualism and collectivism. And Western history from antiquity to modern times provides a rich record of this curious pendulum. It was, after all, the intensive strife between competitive and cooperative value systems besetting Greek society toward the end of the fifth century B.C. that begot the discipline of political philosophy, as Arthur Adkins has reminded us.[1] The rise of cities and commerce necessitated that the purely rivalrous, warlike attitude toward others hitherto

---

1. Arthur W. Adkins, *Merit and Responsibility: A Study in Greek Values* (Oxford, 1960).

dominating the Homeric world be supplemented by quiet values fostering the social cohesion for which Plato's *Republic* makes the most sustained argument.

Within this historical context, Lockit's trope harks back to a pre-Platonic, agonistic model of behavior. Man is above all a predator, albeit one perversely yearning for the company of his potential victims. John Gay's bias reflects, in general, the fraying of the social fabric in early-eighteenth-century Britain and, in particular, the effects of this development on Gay's own predicament. "Political life in England in the 1720s," writes E. P. Thompson,

> had something of the sick quality of a "banana republic." This is a recognized phase of commercial capitalism when predators fight for the spoils of power and have not yet agreed to submit to rational or bureaucratic rules and forms. Each politician, by nepotism, interest and purchase, gathered around him a following of loyal dependents. . . . The great commercial interests (whether in merchanting or finance) depended also upon political and military favours, and these could be paid for at a high rate.[2]

Gay's personal experience with the emerging market economy was unpleasant enough. He was "bubbled" out of his money in 1721 when the South Sea Company scheme collapsed, was deprived of royal patronage in the subsequent political turmoil, and so eventually had to rely on the pen as his primary means of livelihood.[3] The framing of *The Beggar's Opera* (1728) brings its author's dependent economic status to the fore. The Poet is introduced as the Beggar, who in the penultimate scene must reprieve Macheath in order "to comply with the Taste of the Town," lest, of course, he is willing to go hungry.

A phrase in the subtitle of William Empson's influential essay on Gay's play—"the Cult of Independence"—flags the individualistic ethos underlying this work. The desired exemption from control by others (I realize I am oversimplifying Empson's views) can be attained in two ways: through birth or by

2. E. P. Thompson, *Whigs and Hunters: The Origin of the Black Act* (New York, 1975), pp. 197–98.
3. See David Nokes, *John Gay: A Profession of Friendship* (Oxford, 1995), pp. 288–321, 401–8.

entrepreneurship. And the *Opera* pits against each other the corresponding sets of values associated with the gentry and the merchant class. Macheath's aristocratic code of honor is the background against which the mercantile principles of Peachum and Lockit—representatives of the rising bourgeoisie—look particularly unpalatable. The point of Gay's play, however, is not to extol the virtues of refined nobility at the expense of crass capitalists. In an all-pervasive game of double irony (what Empson calls "Comic Primness") values are turned upside down, simultaneously upheld and debunked; this combustible mixture produced a vehicle of social satire. To compare highwaymen to gentry surely renders robbers no less laughable than the aristocracy odious. At the same time, the play makes amply clear that the noble principles guiding Macheath's behavior are just pretense and that they can be flouted for convenience's sake. Mutatis mutandis, we might despair at Peachum's and Lockit's cynical conviction that any selfless feeling toward others, whether loyalty or love, is just another commodity from which gain may be realized. But then our jeremiad should not be directed at these two characters alone. There are enough hints throughout the *Opera* to make viewers aware that others, Prime Minister Robert Walpole most notably, are equally mercenary in their handling of public affairs. And despite all the contempt one might harbor toward Peachum for his unabashed selfishness, there is also something admirable about this "hard-working" criminal, if only the disarming candor with which he speaks of what motivates him.

Given all the complexities of the environment that generated *The Beggar's Opera*, a discerning reader might begin to wonder how, or whether, this play can be transplanted into an altogether different milieu, like the socialist Czechoslovakia of the mid-1970s. This is very much the question lurking behind Empson's somewhat snobbish assertion that caps his analysis of Gay's renowned work: "It is a fine thing that the play is still popular, however stupidly it is enjoyed."[4] Yet, as if to muddy the waters, other critics were much more sanguine about the text's ultimate portability—like Jonathan Swift, who from its inception credited his friend's *Opera* with a robust satirical

---

4. William Empson, "*The Beggar's Opera*: Mock-Pastoral and the Cult of Independence," in *Some Versions of Pastoral* (London, 1935), p. 250.

potential far exceeding that implicit in its original setting. "This Comedy contains likewise a *Satyre*, which, it doth by no means affect the present Age, yet might have been useful in the former and may possibly be so in Ages to come. I mean where the Author takes occasion of comparing those *common Robbers to Robbers of the Publick*, and their several Stratagems of betraying, undermining, and hanging each other, to the several Arts of *Politicians* in times of Corruption."[5]

Let us not, however, get bogged down here in the hermeneutic quicksand of reader-oriented criticism. The question whether a literary text permits only one correct interpretation or whether every reading is necessarily a misprision is not, after all, entirely apropos in a case that looks more like miswriting than misreading. Though Havel's work is indeed called *The Beggar's Opera*, its subtitle, *A Play in Fourteen Acts on John Gay's Theme*, makes it obvious that the Czech author took certain liberties with his venerable source. It is not only his "re-acting" of the original (Gay was content with just three acts, each consisting of thirteen to seventeen scenes) that catches one's eye. Gone are the many ballads sung by the major characters that both imitate and parody the Italian opera so fashionable in Gay's lifetime. Also gone is the meta-theatrical frame through which the Poet-cum-Beggar introduces his creation and, to comply with the generic expectations of his audience, reprieves the condemned Macheath. In the absence of such crucial structural components, why does Havel still call his piece *The Beggar's Opera*? More about this later. And instead of Gay's happy ending—the mock wedding of Polly and Macheath—the Prague playwright opted for a conclusion of his own, which by sleight of hand radically reverses what otherwise seems a straightforward denouement.

To forego his other, less conspicuous departures from Gay's source, Havel's most significant alteration of the text is linguistic. Or, at least, so he assesses his authorial contribution in a letter to the stage director Andrej Krob (to whom the *Opera* is dedicated) critiquing a rehearsal he has just attended. "I was concerned—and the entire play is based on [this principle], which ei-

---

5. Jonathan Swift and Thomas Sheridan, *The Intelligencer*, ed. James Woolley (Oxford, 1992), pp. 64–65.

ther makes it or breaks it—to create a peculiar tension between the 'baseness' of what is spoken about and the 'high language' of how it is spoken about: to wit, that thieves and whores speak like psychologists and sociologists." But it is more than the comical effect derived from the incongruous mesh of obvious incompatibles, Havel hastens to add, that animates his rewrite: "The wit of [my] adaptation neither rests in the traditional story, nor does it exhaust itself in the way the traditional story is inverted, interpreted, travestied, but only in the dialogue through which it unfolds."[6]

So what is so special about the dialogue in Havel's *Opera?* First, the nimbleness with which the characters are able to rationalize any action they undertake, regardless of its unethical nature. Second, the speed with which they are willing, time and again, to reverse themselves, to assume a position that is diametrically opposed to one they just upheld. Folded upon each other, these two signal characteristics of verbal behavior render Havel's dramatis personae rather unpredictable, self-contradictory interlocutors who never mean what they say: their interaction is the comedy of the absurd. One may only wonder why the protagonists even bother repeatedly to justify their unscrupulous behavior if they keep changing attitudes at such extravagant speed. Why, say, does Jenny feel compelled to explain to the jailed Macheath her reasons for delivering him into the hands of the police twice before? Is she, at last, manifesting that modicum of sociability with which Gay's Lockit credited human predators? It does not seem that way! Rather, hers is an exploitative maneuver, using language for a very particular goal: to regain Macheath's affection and to learn (on behalf of Lockit) his secret plan for double-crossing her master, so that it may be foiled. The discourse of Havel's characters, I would argue, is governed above all by strategic considerations. Let me explain.

Under normal circumstances, students of language maintain, speaking to others is a joint venture. We share with our interlocutors a common aim or identify with each other's interests and, thus, regard our exchange as mutually beneficial. Such cooperation is possible because both parties conduct their

6. The letter is dated 24 April 1975; I obtained a copy of it through the courtesy of Mr. Krob. All translations from Czech are mine unless otherwise stated.

conversations according to certain implied principles. Contributions are assumed to be not only sincere but also relevant, balanced as to the amount of information tendered, and unambiguous.[7] One doesn't require the proverbial weatherman to figure out that Havel's dialogues are anything but genuine exchanges of information between equal parties that are rewarding to the participants. Instead, they are semiotic power games in which language serves, first and foremost, as an instrument of coercion, seduction, and manipulation; of covering, uncovering, and counter-uncovering,[8] to mention just a few of its most striking functions. It would be utterly foolish to adhere to any shared conversational principles within a situation where all cooperation is a priori suspect. Sincerity is a fatal weakness—the "honest" pickpocket Filch learns the hard way—and relevance is irrelevant unless, of course, persuasive or to the speaker's advantage. The soul-searching monologues through which the protagonists convey to others their innermost convictions are longwinded, so it seems, precisely in order to prevent others from asking probing questions that might undermine the veracity of their statements. All is equivocal here, nothing can be disambiguated, and the dialogue between the Lockits with which the last scene culminates only reaffirms this fact. The dog-eat-dog world projected by Havel's rendition of *The Beggar's Opera* lacks a privileged vantage point from which perspective the ulterior motives of individual participants might be properly assessed, the manifold layers of their mutual deceptions sorted out, and a definitive winner of this mind-twisting contest for the control of others declared.

Like its eighteenth-century source, Havel's version of *The Beggar's Opera* draws on the individualistic, competitive aspect of human nature and ampli-

---

7. H. P. Grice, "Logic and Conversation," in *Syntax and Semantics: Speech Acts*, vol. 3, ed. Peter Cole and Jerry L. Morgan (New York, 1975), pp. 41–58.

8. The term is Erving Goffman's. He describes the "counter-uncovering move" as purposely furnishing unwitting opponents with the evidence that *they* are seeking to gather through an "uncovering move," but furnishing evidence that is faked in order to confuse them. "The best advantage for the subject," Goffman concludes, "is to give the observer a false sense of having an advantage—this being the very heart of the 'short con'" (see his *Strategic Interaction* [Philadelphia, 1969], p. 20).

fies it into truly grotesque proportions. But is this just a self-contained aes-
thetic exercise along lines furnished by the dramatic conventions of the theater of the absurd, or is Havel trying—as if validating Swift's clairvoyance—to
capitalize on the satirical possibilities of Gay's play to address the foibles of his
own society? The Czech author, for rather obvious reasons, is quite defensive
on this issue. As he vehemently insists in his "Facts about the Performance of
The Beggar's Opera" from April 1976, "In the text of my play one cannot find
anything directed against our state, its regime, or public morality."[9] Very
much like Gay himself in a letter to Swift just two months before the premiere
of his *Opera* some 250 years earlier: "I am sure that I have written nothing
that can be legally supprest."[10] Yet, despite such protestations, both authors
incurred the wrath of those in power. Which is more or less understandable in
Gay's case. His pointed allusions to Sir Robert Walpole were resented by the
subject of his ridicule, as were his suggestive parallels between "common
Robbers" and "Robbers of the Publick," by the Whig political establishment.
But was there anything as offensive to the Czechoslovak authorities in Havel's
play? Indeed there was—the very fact that it was publicly staged, to start with.

The Warsaw Pact invasion of 1968 marked a thorough transformation of
Czechoslovak social and political life. "August of 1968," Havel recollected some
eight years later, "was not just a usual replacement of a more liberal regime by a
more conservative one, it was not just the traditional tightening up after a relax-
ation—it was much more: the end of an era, the disintegration of a spiritual and
social climate, a profound mental hiatus."[11] It took the Soviets some time before
a dependable government could be fully vested in office, but by April of the next
year the process of "normalization" (an official euphemism for reinstalling the
Communist Party's absolute political power) was finally unleashed at full force
upon the local population. Systematic purges of those who mistook Soviet-led
"fraternal help" for military occupation, the wholesale destruction of culture,

9. Václav Havel, "Fakta o představení *Žebrácké opery,*" in *Eseje a jiné texty z let 1970–1989.
Dálkový výslech* (*Spisy,* vol. 4) (Prague, 1999), p. 116.
10. "Gay to Swift, 2 December 1728," in *The Letters of John Gay,* ed. C. F. Burgess (Oxford,
1966), p. 78.
11. Václav Havel, "Dovětek autora ke knize *Hry 1970–1976,*" in *Spisy,* p. 151.

and the raw cynicism of the new rulers—all of these sent a shockwave throughout the society. Havel, along with thousands of other artists, journalists, and scholars, effectively became a nonperson: his books disappeared from libraries, his plays from the stage, and his name from the media.

The Beggar's Opera (1972) was Havel's second play written under these daunting conditions. Unlike his previous works, "It was a new reworking of a classical theme under commission: a certain Prague theater," Havel reports, "commissioned from me a new version of Gay's play, at a time when it still seemed that it could perhaps be staged—somehow."[12] The history of its origin provides a plausible answer to my earlier question: why did Havel retain Gay's original title even though his rendition lacks the Beggar and singing? Because it provided a convenient façade behind which the "untouchable" playwright could hide from the censor's prying eyes. This trick failed in 1972, but the ruse proved adroit three years later when an amateur theater group led by Andrej Krob did its stunt.

Krob met Havel in the early 1960s when Krob became a stagehand at the now famous Theater on the Balustrade in Prague, where Havel himself had been a stagehand for several years. Although Havel had already embarked on his new career as a playwright, he maintained a close working relationship with the Balustrade Theater, and all his pre-1968 plays had their premieres there. But the two men shared more than just a professional affinity. Their summer houses (every self-respecting Czech must have one) in the village of Hrádeček some eighty miles northeast of Prague stood next to each other, and the two neighbors visited frequently, especially in the early 1970s, when Havel, fleeing the inhospitable atmosphere of Prague, made his second home there. This was where Krob, after reading the manuscript of Havel's *Opera*, hatched the plot to stage it. Says Krob: "I enlisted my friends, stagehands and cloakroom attendants from the Reduta Theater [his employer then]. They brought their friends: maintenance men, teachers, white-collar workers, students. Most of them had nothing to do with theater."[13] Rehearsals were held

---

12. Ibid., p. 154.
13. Jana Klusáková, "Andrej Krob: Vším jsem byl rád . . . ," *Mladý svět*, 1990, no. 23:21

in private apartments, country barns, and once even at Havel's summer house in Hrádeček. The morale of the troupe was apparently high, and only one of about twenty actors quit the project, for fear of reprisal from the authorities. The date of the premiere was eventually fixed for Saturday, 1 November 1975, at the House of Culture —known better as the pub At the Čelíkovskýs's (i.e., formerly belonging to the family of Mr. and Mrs. Čelíkovský)—in the remote Prague suburb of Horní Počernice.

This strange choice had several advantages: the distant locale was less likely to attract the unwanted attention of the omnipresent secret police. But more important, the actor playing Macheath, Viktor Spousta, had previously organized several amateur productions in Počernice and was therefore known to the local authorities, whose permission was required for the event to take place. It is not entirely clear how they were bamboozled into granting it. According to Spousta, "I told them that our amateur group had prepared Brecht's play *The Beggar's Opera* [i.e., *The Threepenny Opera*], but that it had been rewritten somewhat because we couldn't do the singing parts. Obviously, I didn't wave in front of them who had rewritten it."[14] But Krob remembers differently. "In our application," he claims, "we listed all the facts correctly, including the author's name."[15] When I asked him in January 2000 how this was possible, he laughed sardonically. The information embargo against Havel, he explained, apparently had worked only too well, and the local officials did not have the foggiest idea who he was. Whatever the actual reason, permission was granted under two conditions: the event could not be advertised, and no admission fee could be charged. The organizers were more than happy to oblige.

Three hundred friends privately invited to see the play had a hard time finding the obscure site of the premiere. It was quite comical, the wife of a prominent dissident who was in attendance told me: a number of cars were cruising around Horní Počernice at dusk, but no one dared stop and ask for directions for fear that the event might be compromised. And Krob cleverly

14. Vladimír Kovařík, "Světová premiéra v Horních Počernicích," *Mladá fronta: Příloha víkend,* 31 March 1990, p. 5.
15. Klusáková, "Andrej Krob," p. 20.

1. The House of Culture in Horní Počernice, where the premiere took place.

incorporated the audience's all-pervasive apprehension into his production of *The Beggar's Opera*, opening it with an act not envisioned by its author. This is how John Kean, with a penchant for the dramatic, describes Krob's creative improvisation that occurred just when everybody expected the performance to start:

> A tall man with a menacing face stepped front stage from behind the drawn curtain. Artfully, in slow motion, he lit a cigarette, which glowed brightly in the darkness of the makeshift theatre. . . . The speechless man carefully aimed

2. Havel arrives for the premiere.

a smoke ring in [the audience's] direction, then began eyeing them
defiantly. . . . He stared coldly at each person below and beyond the stage, beginning with the first row and working his way gradually sideways and back-
wards, one person at a time. . . . By the time the third smoke ring circled over-
head, everybody present had the feeling that something was amiss. It seemed
that trouble had entered the theatre—even that they might well each have to
pay a heavy price for choosing to drive to Horní Počernice. . . . The man com-
pleted his sinister inspection, then slipped silently behind the curtain. Time
seemed to stop, as if fate's turn had now come. The hearts of the audience

3. The hall before the performance.

thumped. Their brows sweated, their bottoms remained riveted to the creaky chairs.[16]

This curious "inspector" was none other than Krob himself. And if his action brought into the open what would otherwise have remained hidden in the viewers' minds—the fear of secret police presence in their midst—they could have relaxed. Miraculously, there were no secret police on the premises that evening.

16. John Kean, *Václav Havel: A Political Tragedy in Six Acts* (London, 1999), p. 235.

4. Renáta Wernerová *(left)*, playing Ingrid, and Zina Kusczinská *(right)*, Betty, preparing for the show.

The show was a great success and the entire crew, together with the elated Havel, retired afterward to the downtown pub At the Little Bears (just around the corner from Prague Police headquarters) to celebrate a job well done. Nothing happened for the next couple of days, and it almost seemed that a second performance announced for the coming Saturday might take place. It was Radio Free Europe that scooped the story on Tuesday, followed by an eye-witness account of the event in the respected West German weekly *Der Spiegel*. The state security apparatus and its Party bosses were enraged. And justly so! If three hundred people (some of them infamous dissidents) could

5. Havel *(left)* and Andrej Krob, the stage director, confer before the premiere.

gather in Prague to watch a public performance of a banned playwright's work, with those in charge learning about it only through foreign media, something must be seriously wrong. So the police, not believing that they could have been hoodwinked by a bunch of amateur actors, began to interrogate the perpetrators of this spectacular monstrosity together with its "innocent" viewers. But no sinister plot "organized from abroad" was discovered and the "culprits" insisted sensibly that they did not break any existing laws. A further complication was that just three months earlier the Czechoslovak government had ratified the Helsinki Agreement, which obligated it (however vaguely) to protect the basic human rights of its citizens. Moscow, for whom this document meant above all Western acquiescence to its post–World War II western frontiers, would not be very pleased, its Prague vassals realized, if one of the satellites openly ignored this hard-won treaty so early after its inception just because a few amateur thespians staged, in the middle of nowhere, a rendition of an eighteenth-century British play. But, at the same time, Czechoslovak officeholders knew only too well that the local population would interpret any passivity on their part as a sign of weakness. And they knew equally well that it was not popularity that kept them in power but their ability to keep everybody under firm control. So they had to act.

Act they did, but in that curiously perverse manner so characteristic of the era aptly dubbed by local wags "Stalinism with a human face." The party ordered its minions to do the hatchet job: fire the participants in the Počernice affair, they were told, but do not ever mention the true reason for the ouster. The case of Andrej Krob, who returned to the Balustrade Theater in 1975 as its chief stage technician, is quite instructive in this respect. At the beginning of the scandal, the director of the theater, Jan Vodička, dismissed him summarily without cause and barred him from the theater's premises. Krob's contract, however, was quite precise as to the reasons for which it could be terminated and, lo and behold, none applied. Despite all the pressure from many corners he refused to quit, was eventually allowed to return to the theater, but was demoted to the position of stagehand. He was actually fired in June 1976, when his job was eliminated as part of the overall "restructuring" of personnel. Needless to say, none of his coworkers were affected by this "streamlining." The final paragraph of the letter that Krob sent to Vodička, who had signed his pink slip, and to the theater's trade union organization, who, as mandated by law, had authorized it, is quite revealing if read against the backdrop of Havel's *Opera*. It illustrates that the theme of double-talk so crucial in the play was definitely more than just an autotelic theatrical device: similarly duplicitous language, it reveals, was quite common among theater administrators as well.

> I am not interested in who in fact was the initiator of this little "witch hunt." Nor is it important how those who signed my dismissal and agreed to it will excuse

their unjust act to others or to themselves. There are people who are always able to interpret weakness and cowardice as goodwill to help others, the theater or the company, as a necessity that came "from above," as their helplessness vis-à-vis somebody else's stubbornness. They simply jumble words: they call the wronged one uncooperative, pusillanimity a tactic to save others, weakness the necessity to follow orders. These are just labels that will not last. But signatures remain forever. As do the patent injustice and cravenness behind them.[17]

There is still one question that remains unanswered. On the one hand, the individualistic tenor of Gay's *Opera* seemed to dovetail well with eighteenth-century England and its spirit of rising capitalism that made the pursuit of self-interest so much a feature of the times. Havel's socialist homeland, on the other hand, seemed, at least from the Western vantage point, a paragon of collectivist mentality. So how could the consummate egoism of his characters have related to the communitarian spirit of a society proud at having eliminated all forms of economic competition? From within, however, communist Czechoslovakia seemed much less a happy family. Witness a popular wisecrack circulating in Prague a few decades ago putting the two seemingly incompatible economic systems—the bourgeois and the proletarian—on equal footing: "Under capitalism, man exploits his fellow man, whereas under communism it's the other way around."

Levity aside, why did the local population not regard their socialist motherland as a beacon of enlightened altruism? Collectivistic societies integrate their members into strong, cohesive in-groups by providing them with cradle-to-grave protection in exchange for unquestioning loyalty.[18] In theory, the Czechoslovakia of yesteryear exemplified such a social contract: citizens who pledged their political allegiance to the state were supposed to obtain from it full economic security. The only problem was that in real life this symbiotic arrangement has never worked too well. The inexpensive goods and services the state had to offer to its consumers were forever in short supply and con-

---

17. The letter is erroneously dated 8 June 1976: it is a reply to a letter of 28 June; I obtained a copy of it through the courtesy of Mr. Krob.
18. Geert Hofstede, *Cultures and Organizations: Software of the Mind* (New York, 1997), p. 51.

sidered inferior in comparison to what was available in adjacent capitalist countries. Even the care delivered by the vaunted national health system was shabby, unless the right palms were greased. The loyalty of the citizenry, in turn, reflected their general dissatisfaction with the system. News coming from the closely controlled official media was discounted in advance, and antigovernmental anecdotes became an indispensable part of the local folklore. State property was pilfered with abandon, and labor discipline was dismal. The ubiquitous summer houses were built mainly from material "liberated" from the state and, in part, during hours when laborers were supposedly working for the "only company in town." True, employment was lifelong and one could get away with doing very little, but then salaries were low and the local money unconvertible. It had to be exchanged illegally (at a very steep rate) for special coupons valid in a few state-run hard-currency stores if coveted Western products were to be procured. Barbed wire along the borders and trigger-happy border guards served as a powerful deterrent against the commonsensical idea of going on a shopping spree abroad just by oneself.

The deep-seated misgiving that the government asked for too much while delivering too little was one reason why ordinary Czechoslovaks did not identify wholeheartedly with their socialist state. Another was the highly inequitable distribution of political power. The post-invasion "normalization" of the country meant, above all, the concentration of the decision-making process in the hands of very few and the full disenfranchisement of the rest of the people. In and of itself, I would stress, the wide gap between the rulers and the ruled need not have split the nation if legitimized properly. Powerless subjects might willingly rally behind a capricious and arbitrary dictator for a number of reasons, charisma being the simplest. The original production of Gay's *The Beggar's Opera*, Empson pointed out, exemplifies well how an unexpected feeling of togetherness can suddenly be stimulated in a country with a high degree of social disparity. By parodying a genre of pastoral that draws a parallel between "low" and "refined" people, the *Opera* served as a cement binding together the disjointed strata of British society. His emphasis on the common human lot enabled Gay's mock-pastoral to break through the rigid class system and, in a curious twist, promulgate national unity rather than divisiveness.

To marshal a nation behind a government propped up by foreign tanks seems a more challenging task, though. And the new party boss, Comrade Gustáv Husák, with his stiff and dour demeanor, could not rely on personal charm either. So he and other Moscow compradors packaged subservience to their Kremlin masters into the timeworn utopianist wrapper of Marxism-Leninism and invoked its logic as the reason why their fellow citizens should follow them. History marches unswervingly toward a bright future, they were never tired of repeating. If not we, our children for sure, will live in the class-less communist Elysium. Hence it was the internationalist duty of other socialist states to help Czechoslovak proletarians (distraught in 1968 by a few perfidious revisionists) to stay this preordained course. And the new government would guarantee their never straying again. I will spare my readers other shibboleths with which the Czechoslovak media relentlessly bombarded the local population in the 1970s to provide Husák's puppet government with the fig leaf of legitimacy. Did anybody take all this seriously? Most likely not, but it really did not matter. The party did not care if the citizens actually believed its ideological gobbledygook. It more than sufficed that they pretended to do so. And the mighty, repressive mechanism at the party's disposal guaranteed that nobody would dare step out of this frame.

The unequal power arrangement between the ruling clique and common Czechoslovaks seems to fit well the parameters of a peculiar hierarchical relationship for which Gregory Bateson coined the widely used label "double bind."[19] Something curious happens to human communication when the figure of authority compels a subordinate to act in a certain way, all the while insisting that the subject of coercion is free or that the enforced behavior is beneficial for him or her. The object language (the content of communication) becomes hopelessly entangled with the metalanguage (the social context in which it occurs), and an assertion made at the primary level contradicts that made at the secondary—as in Epimenides' paradox (a must of every textbook on logic) where the speaker identifies himself as Greek only to confound us by adding that all Greeks are liars. The way out of this trap is to reach yet a higher

19. Gregory Bateson, "Toward a Theory of Schizophrenia," in *Steps to an Ecology of Mind: Collected Essays in Anthropology, Psychiatry, Evolution, and Epistemology* (New York, 1972), pp. 201–27.

level of abstraction from which the knot binding together two incompatible strata of discourse can be cut and the contradiction thereby created, resolved. But this is not always possible in real life, either because of a specific mind-set (for Bateson, schizophrenia is a logical-typing deficiency preventing one from assessing correctly the level of abstraction of a given utterance) or a social pathology. Which brings me back to Havel.

His essay "The Power of the Powerless," written some three years after the Počernice incident, focuses sharply on the double-bind communicative pattern that Havel had been observing daily in his home town. Why, he asks does "the manager of a fruit-and-vegetable shop place in his window, among the onions and carrots, the slogan: 'Workers of the world, unite!'"? This action seems incomprehensible, he is quick to add, only if we do not decipher correctly what is actually being communicated through it. The greengrocer, obviously, has no interest in the tenets of historical materialism. The exhibited slogan is nothing else but a ready-made phrase prepared for this occasion by the Party propagandists, and the merchant only *pretends* to identify with it. By putting it on a display in his window he is signaling, above all, his public surrender to the government (who, after all, owns every store in the country, not to mention everything else), which ought to buy him a peaceful, unmolested existence. He has been bullied into submission, which he may not like, but the merciful Party has gently dressed his wounds with the Marxist-Leninist ideological nostrum. This scientific elixir (which must be neither stirred nor shaken) enables the Party to *pretend* that it is sincere, and the grocer, to *pretend* that he takes this sincerity claim at its face value.[20]

But this convenient pact, to push Havel's idea a bit further, turns sticky when the same grocer faces his children, wife, or trusted friends. Who would like to seem, in the eyes of this innermost circle, a wimp and a doormat? Hence a face-saving explanation of submissive behavior is usually proffered. In the safety of his home the store manager reveals to his closest confidants that by manifesting overt signs of loyalty to the state he was, in fact, *pretending to pretend*, a clever camouflage that gave him the chance to pursue various

---

20. Václav Havel, "The Power of the Powerless," in *Open Letters: Selected Writings, 1965–1990,* trans. Paul Wilson (New York, 1991), pp. 132, 136.

covert schemes serving his private interest alone. True, some party cadres can be fooled for some of the time, but the whole party not for a single second—especially one as paranoid as the CPCS. So to separate grain from chaff, an armada of secret agents is sent out, who by *pretending to pretend to pretend* insinuate themselves into the Machiavellian greengrocers' trust to entrap them, thus exposing their true colors. The wily culprits, however, do not have to go to jail for their disloyalty. By accepting the noble mission of spying on other meta-pretending fruit-and-vegetable shop managers, they can instead atone for their unworthy behavior and help class justice triumph.

The chain of deception characterizing Czechoslovak society in the not so-distant past does not end at this level. Public records furnish examples of pretending that are so multilayered and so fraught with ambiguity that they make Havel's *Opera* look like a realistic piece. Witness the case of "Captain" Pavel Minařík—a broadcaster in the Czech section of Radio Free Europe in Munich—who in January 1976 re-defected to his homeland to the great fanfare of all media throughout the Communist bloc.[21] This 1968 refugee, the world learned from many channels, was apparently a mole planted by state security in the midst of the country's political émigrés to keep an eye on them. But the purely personal reasons behind Minařík's unexpected return (reported by his coworkers), coupled with the paltry trove of compromising materials that he was able to bring back, suggested to many that the official account of this successful intelligence operation was somewhat contrived, to say the least. Whether credible in its entirety or not, the story was released, nonetheless, with a single purpose in mind: to divide and conquer. An increase in the fear-feeding communicative confusion among Czechoslovaks at home and abroad was the best safeguard the Communist Party had to prevent enemies of the state from uniting in sufficient numbers to pose a credible threat to its absolute political hegemony.

Returning now to Havel's play, I hope I have shown that the exacerbated individualism it represents was not entirely alien to the social climate of the

---

21. The collected interviews of this motley figure, Kapitán Pavel Minařík, *Návrat rozvědčíka* (Prague, 1976), were edited by a team of experts from the Czechoslovak Ministry of the Interior; fifty thousand copies have been printed.

6. Havel just before the curtain rises.

country for which it was written. But it is my strong suspicion that its author's aim was not simply to bring to the stage the patent absurdities of the double-bind discourse witnessed around him (though, I must admit, it provided excellent material for a postmodernist artistic sensibility). For better or worse, Havel has always been a socially engaged moralist, a fact that his many essays and, above all, his public life clearly attest to. As such, he considered "the lives within the lie" that most of his fellow Czechoslovaks were content to lead not only demeaning but, above all, self-defeating. Bargaining with the devil (the theme of Havel's 1985 play *Temptation*) cannot end well, even if motivated by the purest of intentions. The ambiguity inherent in a double-bind situation will inevitably sully them beyond recognition. The incessant switching of one's position to satisfy the constraints of ever changing contexts eventually obliterates the distinction between truth and (strategic) lie, means and ends, the dancer and the dance. It creates a moral impasse, quite palpable in socialist Czechoslovakia, where, paradoxically, as Havel observed, "everyone in his own way is both a victim and a supporter of the system."[22] Yet, at the same time Havel was also a skillful playwright with a strong aversion to didactic drama written solely to impart a transparent ideological message. So how did he resolve the eternal dilemma of eating his artistic cake and keeping it socially engaged?

The key to the political reading of *The Beggar's Opera*, lies, I believe, in its finale, the "shocking" dialogue between Mrs. and Mr. Lockit to which I have already referred twice:

> LOCKIT [*putting a serviette in his collar*]. Well, Mary, from this moment on our organization has practically the entire underworld of London under its control.
> MRS. LOCKIT. It took a bit of doing, didn't it.
> LOCKIT. Gaining control of the London Police Force was a piece of cake by comparison.
> MRS. LOCKIT. I still find it strange though, Bill. No one knows about our organization, yet everyone works for it.
> LOCKIT. They serve best who know not that they serve. Bon appétit!

It is not the unexpected revelation that Lockit is a criminal pretending to be a policeman that intrigues me, though. As surprising as this news is, it adds just another step to the ascending ladder of the characters' self misrepresentations unfolding in the *Opera*. Rather, I find telling the pair's smug satisfaction that they won the contest, that in this shadowy game of simulation they were able to dupe all their opponents. Especially when juxtaposed to Lockit's final wisdom concluding the play. In the rapacious universe of his, the latter-day Francis Bacon of the underworld postulates, "Knowledge is power." But with an important caveat: it is the knowledge of other people's intentions that gives one power over them.

22. Havel, "Power of the Powerless," p. 144.

This qualification, however, is what ought to give Lockit heartburn, if not indigestion. For the exclusive source from which he can infer his empowering information—the deliberately misleading signs emitted by his conniving competitors—is precariously unreliable. Furthermore, a double bind situation, is, by definition, communicative confusion. Accordingly, Lockit may never be able to interpret the ongoing exchange correctly: to know for sure whether his triumph is real or assumed, whether he is the master of others or an unwitting servant of somebody seemingly under his control. The text's terminus, I would like to emphasize, does not settle the strategic game that animates *The Beggar's Opera*. It merely demarcates one of the loops comprising the self-perpetuating spiral of mutual deception. That cops might be robbers we learn by the play's end. But we leave Havel's work with the well-grounded suspicion that the opposite—robbers being cops—is more than an idle possibility.

Havel's *Opera* may lack a clear-cut conclusion: Lockit's hubris—inflated self-confidence presaging his eventual downfall—is implied but not actualized, and the protagonist is never castigated. Yet this lacuna does not deprive it of its strong cathartic potential. This is a play about a double-bind predicament written for an audience who knew this situation intimately from everyday experience. By communicating a communicative disorder Havel reframes the double bind of those locked in the primary frame and offers this reframing for their inspection. Presented in its full inner contradictoriness, the game of meta-pretending is portrayed as a vicious circle, a rat race that can be won by none of those who participate in it, whatever their motivation for doing so. From this perspective, then, *The Beggar's Opera* was not merely an artistic imitation of peculiar strategic usage of language existing beyond the stage but also a political gesture: Havel's invitation to his audience to break out of the double bind in which they were trapped, to scrutinize their behavior critically and, if ashamed of what they saw, to change it accordingly. To cease "living within a lie," as Havel articulated such a mental leap, choosing "the life within the truth" instead.[23]

23. Ibid., p. 147.

The Beggar's Opera

To Andrej Krob and his Theater "Na Tahu"

Dramatis Personae

MACHEATH, boss of a criminal organization
WILLIAM PEACHUM, boss of another criminal organization
ELIZABETH PEACHUM, his wife
POLLY, their daughter and Macheath's wife
BILL LOCKIT, Chief of Police
MARY LOCKIT, his wife
LUCY, their daughter and Macheath's wife
HARRY FILCH, a freelance pickpocket
DIANA, owner and operator of a "ladies' salon"
JENNY
BETTY } her employees
VICKI
HAROLD } prison guards
JOHN
JIM } members of Macheath's organization
JACK
A DRUNK
A BARTENDER
THE VOICE OF AN ARISTOCRAT
A SERGEANT
THREE BAILIFFS
INGRID

Scene One

Peachum's household. A spacious drawing room, furnished with solid middle-class taste. A door at the back leads to other rooms in the house. The main entrance is stage right. Upstage there is something like a kitchen nook containing a large stove, various pots and pans, utensils, etc. A large table stands in the middle of the room, surrounded by several chairs. When the scene opens, Mr. and Mrs. Peachum are on stage. Mr. Peachum is seated at the table in a dressing gown, writing something in a large ledger; Mrs. Peachum, in an apron, is puttering around the stove, cooking the noon meal. After a period of silence, Mrs. Peachum speaks.

MRS. PEACHUM: Willy . . .
PEACHUM *not looking up*: What is it?
MRS. PEACHUM: D'you think it was a good idea?
PEACHUM: Do I think *what* was a good idea?
MRS. PEACHUM: That business with Polly and Macheath.
PEACHUM: What about it?
MRS. PEACHUM: I think Polly's going out with him.
PEACHUM: Well, what of it? That was the whole point! *He calls off-stage:* Polly!
POLLY *entering by the rear door:* Yes, Father?
PEACHUM: Is it true you're going out with Macheath?

POLLY: I'm following your instructions, Father. He's invited me out to supper a few times, and I've encouraged his advances, just as you ordered—

PEACHUM: So it's true then? Wonderful, Polly. Keep it up!

POLLY: I'll try, Father. *Exit Polly through the rear door. A knock on the door stage right. Peachum slams the book shut and slides it into a drawer.*

PEACHUM *loudly*: Come in!

FILCH *opens the door and steps in*: Mr. Peachum?

PEACHUM: What do you want?

FILCH: Filch is the name, Harry Filch.

PEACHUM: I've never heard of you.

FILCH: I know. *He looks about the room.* Is it safe to talk here?

PEACHUM: Why shouldn't it be safe?

FILCH: I'm a freelance pick-pocket . . .

PEACHUM: So?

FILCH: These are revolutionary times we're living in, Mr. Peachum—at least as far as our branch of the business is concerned—

PEACHUM: What's that supposed to mean?

FILCH: Cooperation, integration, enormous cartels divvying up the city— small business is having the ground cut out from under it.

PEACHUM: Look, Carnaby Street is all yours, isn't it?

FILCH: In the evenings, Mr. Peachum, there are more of us than shoppers! You can't make it as a freelancer these days, not even if you have the golden touch.

PEACHUM: That's just the trend. It's happening everywhere, division of labor, factories springing up all over the place. You don't expect me to bring history to a grinding halt just because of you?

FILCH: I have a far more modest request, Mr. Peachum.

PEACHUM: What's that?

FILCH: Couldn't you take me on?

PEACHUM: Take you on? We don't even know you!

FILCH: Please, Mr. Peachum, have a heart. If you don't give me a job, I'll be forced to work in a printing shop.

PEACHUM: That's too bad. We don't have any openings at the moment.

MRS. PEACHUM: Why not try Macheath?

FILCH: I'd rather work in a print shop than work for him.

PEACHUM: What have you got against Macheath's outfit?

FILCH: I don't like his methods.

MRS. PEACHUM: I hope you're not just saying that.

FILCH: I'm not, I swear to God, I'm not.

PEACHUM: All right. But I'll have to put you to the test first.

FILCH: Gladly, Mr. Peachum. You're a prince! What do you want me to do?

PEACHUM: Bring me the Duke of Gloucester's watch by tomorrow and I'll consider it. But, don't think you can fool me—I know that watch. And if you get pinched, don't expect me to spring you.

FILCH *rushes over to Peachum and kisses his hand*: I don't know how to thank you, Mr. Peachum.

Filch exits right. Peachum takes the ledger out of the drawer again and begins writing something in it. A short pause.

MRS. PEACHUM: Willy . . .

PEACHUM *without looking up*: What is it?

MRS. PEACHUM: I'm worried.

PEACHUM: What about?

MRS. PEACHUM: About things getting out of hand.

PEACHUM: About what getting out of hand?

MRS. PEACHUM: This business with Polly and Macheath.

PEACHUM: Why should it get out of hand?

MRS. PEACHUM: I think Polly's sleeping with him.

PEACHUM: Well, what of it? That was the whole point! *He calls offstage:* Polly!

POLLY *enters through upstage door:* Yes, Father?

PEACHUM: Is it true you're sleeping with the Captain?

POLLY: Wasn't that what you wanted, Father?

PEACHUM: So it's true then! Wonderful, Polly! Keep it up.

POLLY: I'll do my best, Father.

Polly exits by the upstage door. Someone knocks on the stageright door. Peachum slams the book shut and hides it in the drawer.

PEACHUM *shouts*: Come in!

DIANA *enters through stageright door*: Good morning!

MRS. PEACHUM: Well, well! Diana, it's high time you paid us a visit!

PEACHUM: And how are you, Madam? How's business?

DIANA *sitting down*: Marvelous, Mr. Peachum. The aristocracy's discovered me. A while ago I took on some new talent, all between sixteen and twenty; word got around and now the clients are streaming in. Of course, I raised my prices at once.

PEACHUM: My sincerest congratulations!

DIANA: I must tell you right away that the reason I'm here has partly to do with this new situation. As I'm sure you can understand, what with the social profile of my clientele, I need to redecorate.

PEACHUM: What exactly is it you need?

DIANA: A set of silverware, a few candelabra, and about ten yards of brocade for new curtains.

PEACHUM: You're in luck; it so happens I have as much brocade as you want—

DIANA: Thank you, Mr. Peachum! I knew you wouldn't let me down.

Pause.

MRS. PEACHUM: So, you're doing business with the nobs now?

DIANA: What can I tell you? I've had two dukes, several lords, a bevy of viscounts—

PEACHUM: I had no idea the morals of the upper classes had sunk so low. You're very fortunate.

DIANA: Their morals are the same as they always were; it's just that they used to hush it up. Now, they carry on in public. Mistresses and love affairs have become a sine qua non for upper-class gentlemen. It goes with the territory, like carriages and jewelry.

PEACHUM: How do you explain this shift?

DIANA: Times are changing Mr. Peachum. After all, this *is* the second half of the eighteenth century. In the past, gentlemen became popular and earned the respect of simple people by deeds of valor on the battlefield; today they earn it in the ladies' bedrooms and salons. And who can blame them? It's much more pleasant.

PEACHUM: So you think they're doing it just to be popular?

DIANA: Of course they are! When the man in the street sees that a duke is just a man like himself, made of flesh and blood, with the same passions, vices, and worries, he can't help but feel a certain kinship with him, and he likes him right away. It's a kind of unconscious identification, do you see? But I'm a little surprised—since you're such a wonderful psychologist—that you haven't noticed this yourself and drawn the same conclusions.

PEACHUM: Me? Oh, come on.

DIANA: And why not? These things work the same way in the demimonde as they do anywhere else. As a matter of fact, I would even say that something of the sort should be de rigueur for a man in your position.

PEACHUM: You really think so?

DIANA: Look at Captain Macheath. Why do you suppose he's had such phenomenal success? Why do you think his organization has become so important so quickly? Because he knows how to exploit his erotic scandals to gain public respect.

PEACHUM: But Madam, I'm not Macheath. Sex has never been that important in my life. I'm more what you'd call an intellectual type, and furthermore I have a monogamous temperament. Obviously.

DIANA: Still, there's more than one good joke going the rounds in London about your upright puritanism.

MRS. PEACHUM: Diana's right, Willy. We've overlooked that, and perhaps we were wrong. Shouldn't we put a stop to wagging tongues once and for all?

PEACHUM: It's too late for that, my dear.

DIANA: For some things it's never too late, Mr. Peachum. And besides, you're in the prime of life and if you didn't go around in that moth-eaten housecoat of yours all the time, you could cut quite a figure.

MRS. PEACHUM: Exactly what I've been telling you.

PEACHUM: Don't be ridiculous. As a womanizer I'd be a joke.

DIANA: A successful womanizer is never a joke.

PEACHUM: And what makes you think I could pull it off?

DIANA: Why don't you let me take care of that?

MRS. PEACHUM: Diana knows what she's doing, Willy.

DIANA: Well, I've been in the business for quite some time, you know. I'll pick out just the right girl for you, give her an unpaid leave of absence and some proper coaching—and the rest will take care of itself. You'll see.

PEACHUM: Couldn't we just arrange it so she'd pretend—

DIANA: No, that's not a good idea, Mr. Peachum, not a good idea at all. People—women especially—have a very keen nose for things like that. They'd find out, and it would cause pointless embarrassment.

MRS. PEACHUM: It can't do any harm, Willy.

PEACHUM: Well, if you think so.

DIANA: You agree, then? Marvelous! I'll send you a girl first thing tomorrow on approval. Must run—work calls! Glad I caught you both at home. It's been so nice chatting. You won't forget that brocade, will you, Mr. Peachum?

MRS. PEACHUM: I'll make sure he sends it over, dear.

DIANA: Thank you, sweetie. Bye! Good-bye, Mr. Peachum, and I'll keep my fingers crossed.

PEACHUM: Good-bye.

Diana exits right. Peachum takes his ledger out of the drawer again and starts writing something in it. A short pause.

MRS. PEACHUM: Willy . . .

PEACHUM *without looking up*: What is it?

MRS. PEACHUM: Do you believe her?

PEACHUM: Diana?

MRS. PEACHUM: No, Polly.

PEACHUM: Of course I do. Why?

MRS. PEACHUM: Don't forget, Macheath has a way with women.

PEACHUM: Polly won't fall for his line.

MRS. PEACHUM: What if she already has?

Scene Two

A robbers' tavern: three tables with chairs, a bar in the back, barrels of wine and a door leading to the kitchen. Three steps and a door stage right lead to the street. When the scene opens, Macheath, Jim, and Jack are sitting at one table. A drunk is asleep at another, and will remain so throughout the scene. The bartender shuffles lazily in and out of the kitchen, keeping an eye on things, refilling glasses with wine and disappearing again. Macheath and his mates are in mid-conversation.

JIM: You know what I like most about you, boss?

MACHEATH: What's that, brother?

JIM: Even with all the work you do, and the responsibility of making a go of our organization, you still manage to find time to live a full life.

MACHEATH: Look, it's all part of the same thing. We're successful because I've infused our work with the dynamism of the modern age. We have the daring to tackle grand and unconventional schemes. Could a man with no vitality, no imagination, no spontaneity—in other words, an old geezer like Peachum—carry it off?

JIM: You've even got time for women.

MACHEATH: I have to find time for women, because I am inordinately fond of women. I would even say I'm something of a ladies' man.

JIM: We're ladies' men too. Right, Jack?

JACK: Damn right we are.

JIM: Even though we're not as good at it as you.

JACK: Not even in the same league.

MACHEATH: I don't deny that as a ladies' man, I'm quite successful. Of every ten young women who appeal to me, I usually manage to entice nine into my several beds, sooner or later. And the ones I don't seduce—I don't seduce only because there aren't enough hours in the day.

JIM: Your exploits, boss, are, unfortunately, one of a kind—

MACHEATH: What makes you say that, brother?

JIM: Look at your reputation. You're an outstanding criminal leader, a famous adventurer, a first-rate womanizer, and a man of the world. All that makes it a damn sight easier for you to approach women. Not to mention your other qualities, like your charm and your undeniable good looks.

MACHEATH: Well, yes, of course, my reputation and my generally acceptable looks do, I admit, make things a good deal easier.

JIM: Look at me—with a face like this! I don't stand a chance.

JACK: What about me? Not even a stray dog would go for a kisser like this.

JIM: Just a minute! I'm a lot uglier than you—

JACK: The hell you are!

MACHEATH: You're underestimating yourselves for no good reason, boys. In the first place, you're not that badly off, and in the second place, there are some things more important than good looks. As a crippled friend of mine once said when they didn't want to let him join the gang that gave me my start: beauty isn't everything.

JIM: So what do you think, boss? What does a ladies' man need most?

MACHEATH: What he needs most is that special mixture of insolence, perseverance, humor, and eloquence that characterizes almost everyone who has, as they say, a way with women. You need daring, imagination, and the gift of the gab.

JIM: So what you're saying is that even mugs like us stand a fighting chance?

MACHEATH: Absolutely! And besides, if you think you're not good looking, you can base your strategy and your tactics on pretending to have an inferiority complex. There's nothing a woman likes better than nurturing someone and caring for him—and the more successful she is, the more she loves the man, because through him, she loves her own munificence, of which the nurtured individual is living proof.

JIM: So you think we can turn even our ugliness into an asset?

MACHEATH: Of course you can! And a magnificent asset at that.

JIM: Isn't that something, Jack?

JACK: Oh, I don't know; I think I'd have to give it a try first.

JIM: While we're on the subject of ladies' men, Captain, could I ask you a practical question?

MACHEATH: Go right ahead, brother.

JIM: What do you like better—having your way with proper young ladies or hanging around with experienced courtesans?

MACHEATH: It all depends, my good friend, it all depends.

JIM: Care to be a bit more specific?

MACHEATH: All right. Look, there's a lot to be said for seducing proper young ladies, from that tantalizing uncertainty about the outcome all the way to the fact that it's free. The downside is that seduction can take a lot of time and you have no guarantee of success; furthermore, the girl is inexperienced and seldom able to satisfy you properly. On top of that, there's the constant danger that she'll be charmed by your banter, fall in love with you, and then cling to you like a burr. With whores, on the other hand, you can come to a quick understanding; shame does not prevent them from accommodating your most ardent desires, and they don't clutter up your life with their emotions or demands.

JIM: Whores have been known to—

MACHEATH: Oh, yes, yes, yes—of course. But those are the exceptions: most of the time it doesn't happen.

JIM: What about the downside?

MACHEATH: Mostly that a man who depends entirely on whores in his love life will quickly become emotionally arid.

JIM: So the best thing would be a combination?

MACHEATH: Exactly! And of course you can occasionally spice it up with a third possibility—married women.

JIM *to Jack*: What have I been telling you! And all you ever say is: let's go to the whorehouse and get laid!

JACK: You gotta start somewhere.

JIM: I hope you don't mind all these personal questions, boss.

MACHEATH: On the contrary! I always enjoy shooting the breeze about women in the company of my good friends.

JIM: The thing is, it's invaluable for us to compare our experience with yours. Right, Jack?

JACK: Yeah, sure.

MACHEATH: Go right ahead.

JIM: There's one more thing that interests me: so far, we've been talking mostly about the best way to get women. But isn't it just as important to know how to get rid of them afterward?

MACHEATH: You mean the clingers?

JIM: Right. What do you do with them, for instance?

MACHEATH: There are only two possibilities: either you treat them so miserably that their last shred of pride prevents them from having anything more to do with you, or—the second possibility—you can simply marry them.

JACK: Marry them? That's a good one, boss!

JIM: An interesting concept. But doesn't that cramp your style?

MACHEATH: Quite the contrary, dear brother, quite the contrary! Every serious ladies' man is happily married and some—myself for instance—are even happily married to several women at once.

JIM: I don't get it.

MACHEATH: It's obvious: every woman wants to get married if she isn't already, so the moment you start paying serious attention to her, she begins to regard you as a potential husband. What better way to pacify those demands without resorting to dubious tactics than to point out that you are already married? Your mistress, out of deep regard for the institution of marriage, will feel a kind of sentimental respect for her more fortunate colleague and, in a fit of generosity, surrender any intention she may have had of horning in on her good fortune, provided, of course, that you reassure her, conspiratorially, that your wife is vastly inferior to her, and that this is why you have turned to her instead. In other words, if anything can guarantee a ladies' man reasonable freedom of action, it's a happy marriage. And your regard for your wife's marital happiness will generally be construed in the female world—so full of illusion—as evidence of your respect for the female sex in general, and thus, indirectly, for that member of it who—only because you happened not to have met her first—has been denied marital happiness with you.

JIM: Jack?

JACK: Hmm?

JIM: That's really something, eh?

JACK: He's sure got it worked out.

JIM: You bet. *To Macheath:* I had no idea you were married, Captain.

MACHEATH: In one case, I'm even a newlywed.

Scene Three

The Peachum household again. Everything as in scene 1. When the scene opens, Mr. and Mrs. Peachum are on stage. Mrs. Peachum is setting the table for three. Peachum puts his ledger aside and looks inquiringly at Mrs. Peachum. After a moment, he speaks.

PEACHUM: Liz . . .

MRS. PEACHUM *goes on setting the table*: Hmm?

PEACHUM: What did you mean when you said that maybe Polly's fallen for him already?

MRS. PEACHUM: I don't know why, Willy, but I have a sneaking suspicion that those two have gotten married behind our backs.

She goes to the stove; Peachum jumps up, delighted.

PEACHUM: You don't say! Now wouldn't that be marvelous! *Calls off-stage:* Polly! Polly!

POLLY *enters through upstage door*: Yes, Father?

PEACHUM: Have you and Macheath got married behind our backs?

POLLY: I thought you said it would be the best thing for your business, Father.

PEACHUM: Then it's true? Polly, you're wonderful! Congratulations on a stellar piece of work! Why didn't you tell me?

POLLY: I'm sorry, Father, but things happened so quickly.

PEACHUM: I can see that—faster than I thought myself. Now that you've become Macheath's wife, of course, it's all the more essential for you to understand one important thing. Macheath is undeniably witty, charming and a bit of a celebrity; but there's another, more dangerous side to him. *Meanwhile Mrs. Peachum has served the soup and all three sit down at the table; Peachum tucks his serviette into his collar; they begin to eat.*

POLLY: You're in the same business, aren't you?

PEACHUM: We might be, Polly, we might be, if it weren't for the fact that he has systematically trampled on all the fundamental norms of coexistence between the London organizations, norms that I've worked long and hard to establish.

POLLY: Mack's methods are different, that's all.

PEACHUM: Oh, thank you for pointing that out.

POLLY: What has he actually done to you?

PEACHUM: My dear Polly, there aren't enough hours left in the day to tell you the whole story. The man is constantly undermining my business opportunities and horning in on my markets; he is shamelessly and openly getting rich at my expense; he sets my own people against me, and he's using unethical means to lure the best of them into his own outfit. Isn't that enough?

POLLY: I can't believe Mack is as bad as you say.

PEACHUM: I can name a thousand occasions which prove me right, and everything he does confirms it. He's a rake and a spineless cynic. Why do you suppose he married you, anyway? Because he's scheming to take over my business, that's why. It's pure, cold calculation on his part. But this time, he's come up against a hard rock.

POLLY: Father! Mack married me because he loves me!

PEACHUM: Don't tell me you believe him, Polly!

POLLY: And anyway, if that's what you think of him, then I don't understand why you wanted me to get close to him in the first place.

PEACHUM: Because it's the only way to save our business.

POLLY: So I'm supposed to help bring you two together, is that it?

PEACHUM: On the contrary, my dear Polly. Since you'll be the closest person to him now, I'm counting on you to keep me informed about the state of his organization, what he's up to, his plans. Of course, you can't let him know you're doing it, but that way, I'll finally be able to liquidate his organization, appropriate his holdings, which should belong to me anyway, and gather enough evidence to have him deported for life.

POLLY *stands up*: Father! You can't expect me to betray my own husband!

PEACHUM: Do you want to betray your own father?

POLLY: Well—no—

PEACHUM: So what is it you want?

POLLY: I want to be happily married. I want children. I want to be able to bring them up, to keep house . . .

PEACHUM *smashes a plate on the floor and begins to pace agitatedly around the room*: Happily married? To the biggest whoremonger in London? Keep house? For your father's sworn enemy? And you even want to have his children? Have you taken leave of your senses?

MRS. PEACHUM *sharply, to Peachum*: Willy, just a moment. *Turns to Polly, takes her hand and looks gravely into her eyes.* Polly—

POLLY: Yes, Mother?

MRS. PEACHUM: Tell me the truth now: have you fallen in love with him?

Polly lowers her eyes—a tense pause. Quietly: Polly—daughter—it's not true, is it?

Polly stares desperately at the floor for a moment, then bursts into tears, sits down heavily and covers her face with her hands.

PEACHUM *looks at her in shock, then roars*: Leave my table—you slut! *Polly, weeping and hanging her head, slowly exits through the upstage door. A pause, then Peachum staggers back to the table and sits down, crushed. Another pause. Then he speaks in a broken voice.* This is the worst disappointment of my entire life! My very own daughter! The disgrace! The shame! It's the end of everything!

MRS. PEACHUM: Relax, Willy. Things will sort themselves out.

PEACHUM: How?

MRS. PEACHUM: Radically!

Scene Four

The robbers' tavern again, as in scene 2. When the scene opens, Macheath, Jim, and Jack are still sitting at their table; the drunk is asleep at his. The bartender pops in and out. We find Macheath and his men in the middle of their conversation over wine.

JIM: Listen, boss—

MACHEATH: What is it, brother?

JIM: When you think about it, with your wife's help we could take over Peachum's entire organization.

MACHEATH: That's no way to talk, Jim. Polly's an innocent child. I only married her because she excites me, and because, given my way of life, I need some stability, and that means at least one well-kept household. I refuse to drag Polly into my business.

JIM: Sorry I mentioned it, boss.

The door flies open and a breathless Polly rushes in from the street. Macheath, astonished, gets up.

MACHEATH: What are you doing here?

POLLY: Mack! Darling— *she falls into his arms.* Do you love me?

MACHEATH: Of course I do. What's happened? Won't you sit down? *Polly sinks into a chair; Macheath sits down as well.* These are friends of mine: Jim, Jack—Polly, my wife.

JIM: Pleased to meet you, Mrs. Macheath.

JACK: Charmed.

MACHEATH: Now, what's the matter? You look frightened.

POLLY: An awful thing has happened, Mack. You've got to run away at once.

MACHEATH: Why?

POLLY: My parents are setting a trap for you; they want to send you to the gallows.

MACHEATH: How do you know this?

POLLY: I listened at the door when they were talking about it.

MACHEATH: You did the right thing. What is the trap?

POLLY: I don't know. I wanted to warn you, so I didn't stay to hear the details.

MACHEATH: That was a foolish thing to do. You should have listened to everything.

POLLY: But I was so upset.

MACHEATH: I wonder what's got up their nose all of a sudden?

POLLY: They know everything.

MACHEATH: What do you mean, everything?

POLLY: They know we're married.

MACHEATH: But that was your father's idea in the first place.

POLLY: They also know I love you, and that I'll never betray you.

MACHEATH: What? How did they find that out?

POLLY: I told them.

MACHEATH: Shit! Why did you have to tell them, for Christ's sake?

POLLY: Father wanted me to tell him what you were up to, your plans, so he can destroy your organization, take all your property and have you put on trial.

MACHEATH: But we knew he was after that all along. You were a fool to tell him the truth.

POLLY: But I couldn't promise him I'd spy on you.

MACHEATH: Why not? You can promise anything you want; what matters is what you do afterward.

POLLY: But he said such terrible things about you. He said you'd only married me for your own ends; he said you were out to destroy him.

MACHEATH: Oh, my poor, simple, saintly little girl! You should have agreed with everything he said and promised to go along with him so he'd think his plan was working. And then you'd simply feed him false information, which I would provide, and eventually we'd snare him in his own net. If he trusted you, and thought you were doing just as he wished—and it wouldn't be hard to provide him with false proof of your loyalty—he might even tell you something about *his* plans, and that would be of enormous value to me. But now you've ruined everything!

POLLY: I'm sorry, Mack, but I couldn't deceive my own father.

MACHEATH: You say you love me, but you'd sit back and watch them try to destroy me. That's a strange kind of love.

POLLY: Mack! Mack! I'll do whatever you want.

MACHEATH: It's too late, Polly.

POLLY *bursting into tears*: I don't want to go on living.

MACHEATH: Stop crying! You know I can't stand it when you cry.

JACK: You'd better go to ground, boss.

POLLY *quietly*: Can I come with you?

MACHEATH: Out of the question.

POLLY: What will I do?

MACHEATH: You'll go straight back home, beg your father's forgiveness, tell him you've seen through me and know me for what I am, and promise him that from now on, you'll follow his advice and his instructions because you're convinced he is right and has your own best interests at heart. After that, we'll see—

POLLY: I'll try, Mack. *Polly gets up awkwardly and walks slowly toward the door. She stops and turns to Macheath.* Do you love me?

MACHEATH: Of course.

POLLY: And you'll be true to me?

MACHEATH: You know I will.

POLLY: Always?

MACHEATH: Always.

POLLY: I'll wait for you and I won't think of anyone else.

MACHEATH: Great. Well, so long. *Polly exits through the door to the street.* That's all I needed. Let's go, boys. *Calls off-stage:* Bartender!

The bartender emerges from the kitchen; Macheath tosses him a coin. The bartender catches it and disappears into the kitchen again. Macheath, Jim, and Jack walk upstairs to the door leading to the street. In the doorway, however, they meet Jenny on her way in. Macheath is surprised, and looks curiously at her. She walks down the stairs, Macheath goes slowly back after her. Jim and Jack stand anxiously at the door watching Macheath.

To Jenny: Excuse me, miss, but don't I know you?

JENNY: You remember me?

MACHEATH: Yes, of course. It's just that at the moment I don't know quite where to place you. You don't work in Madam Diana's salon, by any chance?

JENNY: No.

MACHEATH: Then where do I know you from?

JENNY: Do you want to know the truth?

MACHEATH: Indeed I do!

JENNY: Five years ago you robbed me of my virtue.

MACHEATH: Did I really? Tell me, are you still angry with me?

JIM *timidly:* Boss—

MACHEATH *to Jim and Jack:* Go on ahead, boys. We'll meet—you know where. *Jim and Jack look at each other, shrug their shoulders and exit.*

JENNY: I've already come to terms with your deceit.

MACHEATH: I deceived you as well?

JENNY: You promised me love, but when you got what you wanted, you walked away from me.

MACHEATH: I did that? Oh, it grieves me to hear this.

JENNY: It was my mistake. I should never have believed you.

MACHEATH: But I still don't understand how I could have walked away from anyone as beautiful as you. Weren't you somewhat plainer then?

JENNY: You should be the judge of that.

MACHEATH: You were in love with me, weren't you.

JENNY: Very much.

MACHEATH: Well, that's understandable. After all, I was your first—

JENNY: And last—

MACHEATH: What? Surely you must be joking—

JENNY: I know it's absurd, but I've remained faithful to you to this day. Not out of love—love has long since faded.

MACHEATH: Why then?

JENNY: It would take too long to explain.

MACHEATH: Was it traumatic?

JENNY: Something like that.

MACHEATH: So in fact I've robbed you of five years of your life. It's a good thing we've met again.

JENNY: Why?

MACHEATH: Because now there's some hope I can undo the damage I've caused. Who better to restore you to life than the one who robbed you of it in the first place? What did you say your name was?

JENNY: Jenny.

MACHEATH *grasping her by the hand and pulling her to him*: Jenny!

JENNY: Mack! Please! No! No! *Macheath embraces her and begins to kiss her; at first she resists, but her resistance melts: they embrace, kissing wildly. Suddenly she calls out:* Help!
A sergeant and three bailiffs burst into the tavern from the street; the bartender emerges from the kitchen; Macheath tries to break free from the embrace, but Jenny holds him fast.

SERGEANT: What's going on here?

JENNY: This man tried to rape me!

SERGEANT *to Macheath*: In the name of His Majesty the King, you are under arrest, sir. Anything you say from now on may be used against you.

JENNY *cries out*: Oh!
Jenny lets go of Macheath and slumps onto a chair. On a signal from the sergeant, the bailiffs grab Macheath and twist his arm behind his back.

MACHEATH *to Jenny:* You should be ashamed of yourself, you whore!

The sergeant and the bailiffs lead Macheath into the street. The bartender shakes his head gravely and disappears into the kitchen. Jenny sits motionless, staring absently in front of her. After a few moments, the drunk suddenly comes to, gets unsteadily to his feet and calls out.

DRUNK: Long live the freedom of the press!

Scene Five

A prison office. Upstage, a door leading to a corridor; stage left, a door to the prison, fitted with a large bolt and a lock. Downstage left, a large stool and armchair; right, a smaller table with an inkwell and a quill on it, and a chair. There are also some shelves with various law books, documents and files, and one or two other chairs. A portrait of the king and queen hangs on the back wall, along with the prison regulations. In the corner is a large laundry basket full of chains and handcuffs. When the scene opens, Macheath is being formally admitted to the prison. He stands in the middle of the room, his hands tied with rope; Harold is standing beside him, taking objects one by one out of his pocket, examining them, calling out a description to John and then placing them in a chest beside him. John is sitting at the small table making a list of the confiscated articles as Harold calls them out. In general, Macheath ignores this business and is talking with Lockit, who is lounging comfortably in the chair behind the large table.

HAROLD: One pocket knife—
LOCKIT: I understand you're famous for your knowledge of the law, Mackie.
  You're undoubtedly aware, therefore, of the punishment for raping a minor.
MACHEATH: The noose.

LOCKIT: Exactly.

HAROLD: One woman's earring—

MACHEATH: But I didn't rape anybody.

LOCKIT: Got any witnesses?

MACHEATH: It's up to you to prove me guilty.

LOCKIT: I have five witnesses who will tell the jury all about it.

HAROLD: One piece of hemp twine approximately eight feet long—

MACHEATH: Paragraph 7, statue number 15 from 1531—the testimony of bailiffs is inadmissible.

LOCKIT: But they weren't bailiffs.

HAROLD: A rasp—

MACHEATH: Who were they then?

LOCKIT: Prisoners.

MACHEATH: Is this meant to be a joke?

LOCKIT: I don't tell jokes, Mackie. They were prisoners dressed as bailiffs. They did it in exchange for a weekend pass.

HAROLD: One Turkish knife—

MACHEATH: You can get yourself into a lot of trouble doing that.

LOCKIT: Their testimony will still be admissible.

MACHEATH: But it will prove that the whole thing was a setup.

HAROLD: One lady's hankie—damp—

LOCKIT: Wrong, Mackie. It will prove I'm short of bailiffs and that I occasionally get prisoners to fill in. At the same time, I'll stress the rehabilitational aspect of this.

HAROLD: One nail—

MACHEATH: In other words, I'm trapped, is that what you're trying to say?

LOCKIT: So it would seem.

HAROLD: One screw—

JOHN: Wood screw?

HAROLD: Right—

MACHEATH: This is a rotten piece of treachery, Lockit! How much did Peachum pay you to do it?

LOCKIT: I beg your pardon! How dare you accuse me of such a thing! In any case, I had no idea there was any friction between you and that old fox, whose turn, by the way, is coming very soon.

HAROLD: One switchblade, curved handle—

MACHEATH: Then why did you do it?

LOCKIT: I've had your organization in my sights for a long time. There's plenty of evidence right over there. I know your modus operandi inside out. The only thing I don't have, unfortunately, is proof.

HAROLD: Three love letters—of erotic content—

LOCKIT: So I had to go at it a little differently.

MACHEATH: Illegally, you mean.

HAROLD: One small sprocket—

LOCKIT: My conscience is clean. Ridding London of a terror like you is doing society a great favor, so how it's done is irrelevant. You deserve to be punished, and in fact all that will happen is that the jury will base its decision on a different charge than should properly be the case.

HAROLD: One lady's garter, partly torn—

MACHEATH: Listen, Lockit—

LOCKIT: Hmm?

MACHEATH: Are you really out to send me to the gallows?

LOCKIT: Absolutely.

HAROLD: One set of skeleton keys—

MACHEATH: Suppose we came to some arrangement?

LOCKIT: What did you have in mind?

MACHEATH: Two thousand.

HAROLD: One locksmith's clamp with a flange—

LOCKIT: Aren't you being a little presumptuous?

MACHEATH: How about three.

HAROLD: One jimmy—

LOCKIT: You should know me well enough by now to know that I'm not interested in your filthy money.

MACHEATH: Then why are you still talking to me?

HAROLD: A dried chrysanthemum—

LOCKIT: It's my custom to give even the worst miscreants a chance to make amends, right up till the last minute—

Macheath's pockets are now empty; Harold makes one last cursory check.

JOHN: That everything?

HAROLD: Seems like it.

MACHEATH: Look, I'll promise to go straight, if that's what you want.

LOCKIT: You can't wriggle out of it so easily. Anyone could rake in a fortune, then go straight on the proceeds. I'd hardly call that making amends.

JOHN *to Macheath*: Sign that for me, could you?

Macheath goes over to John, glances quickly over the list, then takes the quill and awkwardly—because his hands are tied—signs the list. John takes the document, blows on it to dry the ink, then puts it with his other documents and pulls out another sheet of paper.

HAROLD *to Macheath*: Show me your tongue. *Macheath sticks his tongue out at Harold, who examines it and then shouts to John:* Average moisture, ruddy—

MACHEATH: What do you mean by "making amends" then?

LOCKIT: The only way you can make amends for your crimes is by taking an active part in the war against crime.

MACHEATH: I'm sorry, but what makes you think I have the qualifications?

LOCKIT: This may come as a surprise to you, Mackie, but very few people have your kind of qualifications.

MACHEATH: I haven't the faintest idea what you're talking about.

Harold meanwhile has climbed onto the trunk and begun looking carefully through Macheath's hair.

LOCKIT: Allow me to explain: while it's true that I have intimate contacts with the underworld on a practically daily basis, I am, and understandably will forever remain, on the outside, as it were. At the same time, it would greatly simplify my struggle to maintain law and order if I had some kind of support from within, if you get my drift. In other words, I need a man who enjoys the absolute trust and respect of the entire underworld. You see what I'm driving at, I hope.

HAROLD *getting down from the trunk*: No bugs—

JOHN: Height, please—

Harold stands back-to-back with Macheath and compares heights.

MACHEATH: I'm sorry Lockit, but one of the few things we have in common is that neither of us can be bribed. I'd rather hang.

LOCKIT: Doesn't it seem to you that there's a certain distinction to be made between a bribe taken by a man of the law from the hand of a criminal, and the offer of a chance to make amends that a criminal might receive from the hands of a man of the law? The two things are simply incommensurable.

HAROLD: Six feet—or thereabouts—

JOHN *writing*: Weight?

Harold grabs Macheath around the waist from behind and, with great effort, hoists him off the ground.

MACHEATH *dramatically, as he dangles in the air*: A rat is a rat no matter how you look at it!

HAROLD *dropping Macheath*: Hundred and eighty—or thereabouts—

JOHN: Thank you, Harold.

HAROLD: That everything?

JOHN: Yup.

John straightens out his papers and puts them away; Harold unties Macheath's hands and pulls the basket of handcuffs over to him.

HAROLD: Take your pick.

Macheath examines the handcuffs with a practiced eye, trying some of them out.

LOCKIT: Obviously, you want to play the hero, Mackie. Fine, I won't stop you. But don't expect me to admire you either. To my mind real heroism would be making amends for your past and serving a good cause. What you're prepared to do is an empty gesture that no one will understand, that will help no one and will merely cause pain to a few of those closest to you. It will be a typically meaningless death.

MACHEATH: My honor is dearer to me than my life. *Shows Harold the hand-cuffs he has chosen.* These ones.

HAROLD: Those are first-class cuffs.

MACHEATH: What of it?

HAROLD: They cost five pence a day.

MACHEATH: That's robbery!

Harold puts the cuffs on Macheath's hands.

JOHN: It's our only chance to earn a little extra.

LOCKIT: Anyway, Mackie, do what you will. You make your bed, you lie in it. But if you feel inclined to change your mind in the few days you have left, I'm always available.

HAROLD: The hole, boss?

LOCKIT: Of course.

Harold unlocks the door left and leads Macheath away into the prison. John puts the basket of handcuffs back in its original spot, picks up the trunk of things and exits through the back door. Shortly after, there is a knock on the door.

Calls out: Come in.

Peachum enters through the upstage door and walks over to Lockit, smiling. They shake hands.

PEACHUM: I hear you've collared him, Bill.

LOCKIT: He's in cell number six, if you'd like to pay him your respects.

PEACHUM *laughs*: I'll pass.

Peachum makes himself at home on one of the chairs. Harold comes back into the office, locks the door behind him, and leaves through the upstage door.

I'm grateful to you, Bill, for myself and for Liz. This means a lot to us.

LOCKIT: Let me tell you something, Willy: this is the last time. Next time, you can sort out your family problems without my official assistance.

PEACHUM: Anything go wrong?

LOCKIT: No, but I don't like this way of doing things. I don't like it a god-damned bit.

PEACHUM: Just be glad you've got him under lock and key. Or don't you believe he's got some of the biggest heists in recent history on his conscience.

LOCKIT: That's exactly why I wanted to wait until I had the goods on him. Then I could round up him and his whole gang and have a monster trial, put the fear of God into the entire underworld. Now his men will all go to ground and strengthen various minor organizations, or start operating independently—and we'll be right back where we started. And to top it all off, we'll make a romantic hero of him, a victim of a woman's treachery.

7. Andrej Krob *(left)* as Lockit and Jan Hraběta as Peachum.

PEACHUM: I did what I could, Bill. I put my own daughter on the line to get as much proof as we could. It just didn't work out, that's all.

LOCKIT: I'm sorry, Willy, but what did you expect? You know how slick Mack is with women. You should have consulted me first. And besides, it's still not entirely clear to me why you went into such a risky business on your own.

PEACHUM: What are you trying to say, Bill?

LOCKIT: I'm only trying to say that you used to be a lot more careful.

PEACHUM: Even the most faithful servant of the law can sometimes bungle things.

LOCKIT: Let's drop the subject, Willy. It doesn't make any difference anyway. By the way, you wouldn't happen to know who took the Duke of Gloucester's watch, would you?

PEACHUM: Well, well. The fellow actually managed to pull it off.

LOCKIT: You know who it was?

PEACHUM: I was trying someone out.

LOCKIT: That's wonderful. The Duke is fit to be tied. And anyway, how come you're taking on new people?

PEACHUM: It was the only way I could get rid of him.

LOCKIT: Look, Willy. When you put your organization together, we agreed that it would never get any bigger than necessary for the role it was intended to play, which is to establish your credibility within the underworld. Instead, you're expanding your operations. Why? If this keeps up, soon it won't be a front for our work any more and it'll become a dangerous business, one that will ultimately do society more harm than good.

PEACHUM: You're not being fair, Bill. I haven't hired anyone for a year.

LOCKIT: Who did it?

PEACHUM: Can't you pin it on someone else? If you pick him up now, you'll blow my cover.

LOCKIT: Christ, you make things difficult.

Pause.

PEACHUM: Say, Bill—

LOCKIT: Hmm?

PEACHUM: Do you think Mary would like a pearl necklace?

LOCKIT: Now what the hell is that supposed to mean, Willy? As I understand it, you're to turn over all your clear profit to the city treasury.

PEACHUM: I thought we could make a small exception in this case. It's a wonderful little item.

LOCKIT: A wonderful little item! Do you have any idea what you're doing? Surely you're not suggesting that we crime fighters should become criminals?

PEACHUM: Bill! My lowest-ranking pickpocket makes more in a day than you do in an entire month. You call that justice?

LOCKIT: I don't know about you, Willy, but I knew very well—when I went into this trade—that I could expect nothing but ingratitude.

PEACHUM: There you go again, suspecting me of ulterior motives. You're not being fair to me, Bill. Do you know that my profession is one of the few in the world that can't be pursued out of a mere love of profit?

LOCKIT: I'm sorry. I don't mean to offend you. Have you got it with you? *Peachum pulls the necklace out of his pocket and hands it to Lockit who examines it expertly.* Magnificent.

PEACHUM: Isn't it just!

LOCKIT *sticking the necklace in his pocket*: Well, thanks then—

Scene Six

A prison cell. Upstage is a barred window, against the wall, stage right, a military cot; and opposite, a tiny table, stool, and a massive door with a peephole. Macheath, handcuffed, is lying on the cot. A key rattles in the lock and Macheath quickly gets to his feet. Harold enters.

HAROLD: You've got a visitor, Captain.

MACHEATH: I do?

Lucy enters; Harold exits, slamming the door behind him.

Lucy! *Lucy steps up to Macheath and kisses him on the cheek.* What's up?

LUCY: Where have you been?

MACHEATH: Where have I been when?

LUCY: You have to ask? I haven't seen you since the wedding, and that was over a year ago. Do you think marriage is a cage you can just fly away from? What's going on in your mind?

MACHEATH: I can explain, Lucy—

LUCY: I'm listening.

MACHEATH: I stayed away because of you.

LUCY: Because of me? What's that supposed to mean?

MACHEATH: I didn't want to get you into trouble. Do you know what your father would do if he ever found out that we're married?

LUCY: Why don't you come right out and say it: you were bored with me.

MACHEATH: That's nonsense! On the contrary—

LUCY: If you really loved me, you'd have found a way. Why did you marry me in the first place? Go on, tell me. Why?

MACHEATH: I had a plan: I wanted to make a little nest-egg on the quiet so we could move to the country and live together and be happy ever after.

LUCY: You liar!

MACHEATH: It's true, Lucy. In fact, I almost managed to pull it off.

LUCY: That's funny. I never noticed.

MACHEATH: I've almost got the money together. If your father hadn't set that devious snare to entrap me and send me to the scaffold, we could have left in a few days.

LUCY: They're going to hang you?

MACHEATH: Your father says I can absolutely count on it. Lord knows what he's got against me. At first I thought it was because he'd found out somehow about our plans to leave town.

LUCY: How could he have found out when I didn't even know myself?

MACHEATH: Lucy, it's an awful thing, but our happiness was crushed just as it was about to burst into flower.

LUCY: I don't believe you.

MACHEATH: You've got to believe me, Lucy. It's a whole string of unfortunate misunderstandings. If you only knew how much time I've spent thinking about you. Every day, in my mind's eye, I've imagined a small ivy-covered, red-brick manor house in the country, surrounded by green meadows and beech-tree forests, and just the two of us, living together, running through the meadows with our greyhounds, riding on horseback, hunting the noble stag, bathing in a nearby brook, gathering wild mushrooms, preparing meals of old English fare, throwing parties for the local aristocrats, raising sunflowers—and then, in the evening, sitting down before an old Elizabethan fireplace, gazing into the flames, telling each other stories from our childhood, reading aloud from old books, sipping mead—and then, flushed with sweet wine, mounting the stairs to the manor bedroom, the fragrant night air wafting through the window, the voices of a thousand cicadas calling to us from the meadows and the pale light of a million stars softly falling on us from heaven—thus enchanted, we slip out of our clothes and lie down side by side beneath the canopy of a large gothic bedstead, and there we cover each other with long, slow, tender kisses and then we make love, our hot bodies, brown from the sun, mingle and tangle in wild abandon and we clutch and cling in the throes of love, and then, at last, infinitely content and sweetly exhausted, we fall asleep, to be awakened next morning to the sparkling summer sun, birdsong, and the butler bringing us bacon and eggs and cocoa.

LUCY *shouts*: Oh, Mack, stop! *She collapses in tears on the stool and sobs.* It's all lost—all lost!

Macheath steps up to Lucy and grasps her hands in his, though his hands are shackled together.

MACHEATH: Nothing is ever lost, Lucy.

LUCY: What do you mean?

MACHEATH: All that can still be ours—and many other wonderful things as well. It's entirely up to you.

LUCY: Oh, Mack—what can I do?

MACHEATH: Get me a hacksaw.

Scene Seven

The Peachum household again; everything as usual. Mr. and Mrs. Peachum are on-stage. Peachum is wearing a housecoat, sitting at the table and writing in a large ledger; Mrs. Peachum, in an apron, is hovering over the stove preparing the noon meal. After a while, Peachum stops what he is doing, thinks for a while, and then speaks.

PEACHUM: Liz . . .

MRS. PEACHUM *without turning around*: What is it?

PEACHUM: Do you think it was a good idea?

MRS. PEACHUM: Do I think *what* was a good idea?

PEACHUM: Sorting out that business with Macheath so radically.

MRS. PEACHUM: It was the only thing we could have done, Willy.

PEACHUM: And what about Polly? Does she know?

MRS. PEACHUM: No, why?

PEACHUM: I wouldn't want her to do anything rash.

MRS. PEACHUM: What an idea!

There is a knock on the door stage right. Peachum quickly snaps his book shut and hides it in the drawer.

PEACHUM *calls out*: Come in! *Enter Filch.* Ah, Filch, my good man. We've been expecting you. Congratulations!

Filch takes a gold watch from his pocket and tosses it on the table. Peachum picks it up at once and examines it expertly.

MRS. PEACHUM: You're the man of the hour, Mr. Filch.

PEACHUM: That's it, all right. *He puts the watch in his pocket.* A perfect job. Gloucester and Lockit are fit to be tied.

MRS. PEACHUM: To tell you the truth, we didn't really think you could do it.

PEACHUM: Ah, but it was a splendid piece of work. You'll be one of the pillars of my organization.

A pause. Filch looks sullenly at the floor. Mr. and Mrs. Peachum don't know what to say.

What's the matter, Filch, aren't you pleased with yourself.

A pause. Filch looks abruptly at Peachum.

FILCH: Mr. Peachum—

PEACHUM: Yes?

FILCH: Do you mind if I ask you something?

PEACHUM: Go right ahead.

FILCH: You don't happen to know who turned in Captain Macheath, do you?

PEACHUM *caught off guard*: Why, no.

FILCH: Well, I do!

PEACHUM: Who was it then?

FILCH: It was you!

PEACHUM: Me? I beg your pardon, but that's utter nonsense. Who told you that?

FILCH: The Captain himself.

PEACHUM: How could he? He's in prison.

FILCH: He managed to escape last night.

PEACHUM: What?

MRS. PEACHUM: I don't believe it.

FILCH: The word is that Lockit's own daughter helped him get away.

PEACHUM *explodes*: I knew it! I knew there'd be hell to pay.

MRS. PEACHUM: Calm down, Willy.

PEACHUM: You shut your mouth! It's all your fault.

MRS. PEACHUM: Go ahead, blame it all on me. It's a slanderous lie, Mr. Filch, concocted by Macheath just to ruin us.

FILCH: But he has witnesses who say that just before he was arrested, your daughter came to warn him.

PEACHUM: I'll break every bone in her body!

FILCH *delivered as a pronouncement*: Mr. Peachum! I despise you.

PEACHUM *glares at Filch for a moment, then frowns and says wearily*: All right, Filch, I'll tell you the truth. It was me who turned Macheath in and had him arrested. The point is that if I hadn't done it, he'd have done it to me, so in fact it was an act of self-defense. Does that satisfy you?
Filch lowers his gaze and stares thoughtfully at the ground for a moment. Then he turns abruptly to Peachum.

FILCH: Mr. Peachum, you may think this is silly, but to me you were always the very embodiment of the classic virtues of the London underworld, a symbol of our esprit de corps, a boss of the old school with unshakable principles, a sense of fair play, loyalty to others of our estate, someone who would sooner give himself up than betray a colleague and turn him over to the police. Have you any idea how bitterly disappointed I am? My last great ideal has fallen—it was all an illusion, self-deception, a mistake. My world has collapsed.

PEACHUM: Through no fault of mine, Filch.

FILCH: Whose fault is it then?

PEACHUM: Your own.

FILCH: You can't be serious.

PEACHUM: You're living in an ivory tower.

FILCH: Are you trying to tell me I'm out of touch with reality? I, who spend the better part of each day on the street?

PEACHUM: I'm sure you're fine as a petty thief, but—I hate to say this—you haven't a clue how big operations work. If you did, you'd know that no boss of a large organization today can possibly get by without cooperation, of one sort or another, with the police. You'd be very surprised, sir, if you knew all the people from our circles who call on Mr. Lockit every day.

FILCH: I simply don't understand that.

PEACHUM: Do you think my organization could prosper as it does if I didn't put a wall up around it by cooperating with the other side? Don't be naive.

And that's not to mention all the important information I've gleaned that way, all the people I've helped out, all the apparently lost causes I've pulled out of the fire. Isn't that so, Liz?

MRS. PEACHUM: Of course it is.

FILCH: But the price you had to pay for all those achievements—you're not talking about that.

PEACHUM: Of course it hasn't been a free ride; the police aren't that stupid. The only important thing about this game is that the profits should, as far as possible, exceed the losses.

FILCH: I'm sorry, Mr. Peachum, but I find that kind of trafficking with the enemy disgusting.

PEACHUM: Trafficking with the enemy? Perhaps it is. It's a thankless task, sir, but someone has to do it. What would become of the underworld if people like me didn't put their honor on the line each and every day by keeping the channels of communication open, something for which they will very probably never receive proper credit? How do you think you're able to go blithely on, stealing watches from dukes, flaunting your lily-white hands and issuing your simplistic moral edicts? Oh, it's terribly easy to cloister yourself away and cultivate your marvelous principles, but what sense does it make? Only this: it gratifies the egotistical self-interest of those who do it. The real heroes of the underworld today are a different breed of men altogether. They may not constantly flaunt their fidelity to the pure code of honor among thieves, but they do modest, inconspicuous, and risky work in that no-man's land between the underworld and the police. And they make a real contribution to our objective interests. By not hesitating to dirty their hands from—as you put it—trafficking with the enemy, they expand the range of our business opportunities inch by inch, strengthen our security, keep us informed, and slowly, inconspicuously, with no claim to glory, serve the cause of progress. The era of the romantic highwayman of the Middle Ages is long past, sir. The world has changed, other standards have prevailed for some time now, and anyone who fails to understand that has understood nothing. You're still young, Filch, and you're an idealist. I understand that, and despite what you've said, I rather

8. Jan Hraběta *(left)* as Peachum and Jan Kašpar as Filch.

like you. But for that reason alone, let me give you this piece of advice: get rid of your illusions while there's still time. Come down to earth from your ethereal heights, look at the world around you, try to understand it, free yourself from the thralldom to abstract principles! It's in your own interests.

FILCH: I may seem to you like a hopeless crank, Mr. Peachum, but rather than steal under police protection, I'd prefer honest labor.

PEACHUM: So you will go to work in the print shop?

FILCH: Yes.

PEACHUM: Well, make your bed and lie in it! But let me tell you one thing: you'll regret it, and then you'll remember me. Good luck!

FILCH: Farewell, Mr. Peachum.

Filch exits by the door stage right.

PEACHUM: Did you see that? The devil take the fellow! Now he'll be all over London telling everyone I admitted to collaborating with the police.

MRS. PEACHUM: Relax, Willy. It will sort itself out.

PEACHUM: How?

MRS. PEACHUM: Radically.

Intermission

9. The audience at the break.

Scene Eight

Diana's salon. It is a spacious room; the furnishings suggest a pretension of luxury. The main entrance is downstage right. There are two doors upstage and a fourth door on the left. A stairway right leads somewhere above. Downstage center there is a large desk with an armchair behind it and, in front, a small cupboard with keys and a taboret. It is all somewhat reminiscent of a hotel reception area. Upstage is a small table surrounded by several chairs. When the scene opens, Diana is sitting behind the desk talking to Jim, who is seated opposite her on the taboret; he is dressed in a good suit with a boutonniere in his lapel. Betty and Vicki are sitting in the armchairs upstage; Betty is knitting a sock and Vicki is reading.

DIANA: My salon is not large—there are certainly larger establishments in London—but I have deliberately chosen not to expand. I believe that a service of this kind cannot be provided as though it were some kind of assembly-line product, and those large, anonymous establishments that mechanize and dehumanize the whole business, reducing it to the level of mere consumption, simply go against my grain. I'm sure you'll agree that nothing as deeply individual as love can ever be made an object of mass consumption.

JIM: I couldn't agree more, Madam. Everything in the modern age that alienates man goes against my grain too!

DIANA: Quite so! And that is precisely why I try to maintain the family atmos-phere, as it were, of my salon, to keep a small but steady clientele and en-sure that the relationship between my girls and the customers is not just commercial, but above all human.

JIM: Very shrewd of you, Madam. I'm sure that your customers are sincerely grateful.

DIANA: Indeed they are. And now, perhaps it would be appropriate to proceed to your choice of partner for today. Do you agree?

JIM: Of course—

DIANA: In that case, you may wish to consider one of the ladies who happen to be free at the moment—to avoid a possible delay. *Points to Betty.* This is Betty. *To Betty:* Betty, come and show yourself to the gentleman. *Betty puts down her knitting, comes downstage, and begins to turn and assume various poses in front of Jim.* Betty's chief attraction to our customers is an elemental animality in her nature that helps them overcome any possible shyness and the complica-tions that arise, or fail to arise, in terms of their masculinity, if you see my point.

JIM: I think I see your point.

DIANA: In her animality, however, she is not insensitive to her partner's needs; on the contrary, Betty has a subtle grasp of a wide assortment of techniques, and she can accommodate her customer's whims quite spon-taneously, of course, insofar as they do not go beyond what we, in the sec-ond half of the eighteenth century, consider the limits of biological nor-mality. Show the man your legs, Betty! *Betty lifts her skirt and shows her legs.* Pretty, aren't they?

JIM: Yes, very—

DIANA: Would you like to examine her teeth?

JIM: No thanks, that won't be necessary.

DIANA *to Betty:* That will be all, Betty. *Betty goes back to her place and resumes her knitting. Diana points to Vicki:* Now this is Vicki. *To Vicki:* Vicki, come over here. *Vicki puts down her book and comes quickly forward, where she be-gins to turn and pose in front of Jim.* In some regards, Vicki is the precise opposite of Betty. She is high-strung, of a melancholy disposition, a some-what romantic creature with an enormous inner dynamism and a rich emotional life. What customers find exciting about Vicki is her flair for drama and her powerful element of mystery. Vicki is intellectually quite gifted. *To Vicki:* Tell us, Vicki, what are you reading at the moment?

VICKI: Descartes.

DIANA: And what do you think of him?

VICKI: Somewhat prolix—

DIANA: There, you see! Vicki, moreover, has a great many physical assets as well; her firm breasts are outstanding. *To Vicki:* Show the gentleman!

Vicki shows Jim her breasts.

JIM: Smashing—

DIANA: Aren't they? Everyone says so. *To Vicki:* Thank you, Vicki, you may go.

Vicki returns to her chair and goes on reading.

Well, do you think one of the ladies present might suit?

JIM: They're both very desirable.

DIANA: If you'd like both at once, that can be arranged too.

JIM: Really—

DIANA: Well? *A pause. Jim is having trouble making a decision.* Have you made up your mind?

A pause. Jim is still undecided, but finally responds quietly.

JIM: Madam—

DIANA: Yes?

JIM: I don't quite know how to put this, but I think I'd have a better under-standing with you—

DIANA: I beg your pardon? Do you know who I am?

JIM: Excuse me—I only meant to say that we're of one mind as far as Betty's charms are concerned. I'm sorry—

DIANA: That's more like it. Betty! You've got a customer.

Betty puts her knitting down and walks over to the table; Diana leafs through her book, then turns to Betty.

Number ten, all right?

BETTY: Again?

Diana looks at her pocket watch, enters the time in the book, takes a key on a large pear-shaped pendant from the cupboard and what looks like a blank form, and gives them both to Betty.

DIANA *to Jim*: Go to it, handsome!

Betty pushes Jim toward the stairs; Jim mounts them awkwardly with Betty behind him. As soon as they exit, the door stage right flies open and Macheath enters. Diana is upset and jumps to her feet.

You must be our of your mind! Are you trying to get us all arrested? Do you know what would happen if they found you here? I'm directly responsible for these girls to their mothers. You'll have to leave at once.

MACHEATH: Is there someone called Jenny here?

DIANA: Why?

MACHEATH: I must have a brief word with her.

DIANA: Out of the question!

MACHEATH: Don't forget you're directly responsible to their mothers for these girls. The sooner Jenny gets down here, the sooner I leave.

DIANA *shaking her head unhappily and heading for the door stage left*: You're an awful man, Mack! An awful man! *She puts her ear to the door, listens for a moment, then knocks delicately.*

JENNY *off*: What is it?

DIANA: Would you mind, just for a moment?

JENNY *off*: Right this minute?

DIANA: Yes— *She nods to Vicki, looks angrily at Macheath, and exits through the upstage right door; Vicki takes her book and follows her off. Jenny enters through the door stage left. Her hair is disheveled and she is wearing only a peignoir, which she is just doing up. She is startled to see Macheath.*

MACHEATH: Surprise!

JENNY: I was expecting you to come. I have a lot to explain.

MACHEATH: What is there left to explain? That you're working for the police and are willing to do anything they ask? I know that already.

JENNY: You know nothing.

MACHEATH: What do you mean?

VOICE *off*: Pussycat—

JENNY *calling toward the door stage left*: Just a moment—

MACHEATH: So you want me to believe you're not working for the police?

JENNY: I want to tell you the truth.

MACHEATH: You told me the truth in the tavern, too.

JENNY: That was different.

MACHEATH: Tell me about it.

JENNY: If I hadn't tried to give you the impression that I was telling the truth, that little comedy about love betrayed wouldn't have made any sense.

MACHEATH: And they wouldn't have caught me, right?

JENNY: Exactly.

MACHEATH: Fine. Now what's your truth for today?

JENNY: I'm not Lockit's stooge. Nothing is the way you think it is.

MACHEATH: What's not the way I think it is?

JENNY: They forced me to do it, that's all.

MACHEATH: How could they do that?

JENNY: They promised to grant my father a pardon. He's been sentenced to death, you know.

MACHEATH: Your father's been sentenced to death?

JENNY: Yes. It was a terrible dilemma and for a long time I had no idea what to do; I felt I had to refuse, because I couldn't bring myself to save one man from death by sending another to the gallows. In the end, however, I knew you'd find a way out of it, but Father wouldn't. You'd have to know him. He's so defenseless. So I went along with their offer.

MACHEATH: Have they let your father go?

JENNY: Well, not yet, but they haven't hanged him either.

A pause. Macheath is somewhat unsure of himself.

MACHEATH: Very well, but what if all this is just as big a load of rubbish as what you told me back in that tavern?

JENNY: You can check on it, can't you?

MACHEATH: Even if it is true that your father's been pardoned, how can I ever find out if they used that to pressure you into turning me in? No one would ever admit that to me.

JENNY: You see how fiendishly cleverly they are? Oh God, it's all so confused. What should I do, tell me?

MACHEATH: Your only hope is that I'll believe you.

JENNY: I know it's hard—and I could hardly blame you if you didn't.

MACHEATH: Would you at least regret it?

JENNY: I'd be desperately unhappy.

MACHEATH: Really?

JENNY: Really.

MACHEATH: Your conscience would bother you?

JENNY: That too.

MACHEATH: What else?

JENNY *quietly*: I can't tell you.

MACHEATH: Why not?

JENNY: Some other time.

MACHEATH: You're forgetting there might not be another time for me.

JENNY: Don't talk that way, for God's sake!

MACHEATH: I'm a realist.

JENNY: If I could just do something to prevent them from catching you.

MACHEATH: I'll be satisfied if you don't do anything so they will.

JENNY: Do you have to keep on reminding me? Don't you think I knew what I was doing?

Pause.

MACHEATH: Jenny, listen—

JENNY: Yes?

MACHEATH: It's odd, isn't it?

JENNY: What's odd?

MACHEATH: Do you know why I came here?

JENNY: To tell me I was a bitch.

MACHEATH: Yes. And now look—I'm going to leave here feeling that you couldn't help doing what you did, that I should be the one apologizing to you—

JENNY: Oh, Mack!

Jenny grasps Macheath's hand joyfully in both of hers and kisses it. Macheath is momentarily taken aback, then he quickly put his arms around Jenny and begins to kiss her. She puts up a slight struggle.

No, no—please—no.

Jenny surrenders; they kiss passionately for a time, then Jenny tenderly extricates herself from Macheath's embrace, takes him by the hand, and with a shy smile leads him to the upstage left door. She stops in front of it, looks around, and then whispers.

JENNY: Do you want to?

MACHEATH: You're not afraid?

JENNY *shakes her head with a smile*: And you?

MACHEATH: There are times when I'm incapable of thinking about the future.

VOICE *off*: Pussycat! Come back!

JENNY *to the stage left door*: I'll be right with you.

Jenny looks around conspiratorially once more, then quietly opens the upstage left door and quickly pushes Macheath inside. Before the door closes, she signals him through the crack to be silent.

MACHEATH *whispers offstage*: You won't be long?

Jenny smiles at Macheath through the crack in the door, nods and then gently closes the door. She looks around once more, then quietly runs out through the door stage right. Immediately, there is shouting and noise offstage, then an astonished Jim rushes on down the stairs in long underwear. Behind him, an enraged Betty appears, in her underclothes, with Jim's trousers in her hands.

BETTY: Get out of here, you disgusting pervert! Pig!

Scene Nine

The Peachum household again. Everything as usual. When the scene opens Mr. and Mrs. Peachum are onstage. Mrs. Peachum is hovering around the stove; Peachum is sitting at his table, his ledger in front of him.

PEACHUM: Polly!

Polly enters through upstage door.

POLLY: Yes, Father?

PEACHUM *sternly*: I've heard you warned Macheath about our plans. Is this true?

POLLY: Unfortunately, it is.

PEACHUM: Why do you say "unfortunately"? Don't you love him?

POLLY: He deceived me. He told me he loved me, but he was planning all along to use me against you. You were right about everything, and I was a fool to believe him.

PEACHUM: Polly! My sweet girl! So you've seen through him? Splendid! Tell me how it happened?

POLLY: When I was warning him about your plans, I told him I'd confessed to you that I was in love with him, and he got terribly upset with me. He said that I should have kept that a secret and gone on pretending I was seeing

53

him just so I could report back to you, as he wanted. He said if you trusted me, he could use that against you.

PEACHUM: The young man had it all very cleverly worked out.

POLLY: When he let that slip, I realized I'd been deceived.

PEACHUM: And you're sorry?

POLLY: Yes.

PEACHUM: D'you hear that, Liz? The prodigal daughter returns. Come on, give us a hug, Polly!

Polly goes up to Peachum; he embraces her and kisses her.

POLLY: Can you ever forgive me?

PEACHUM: Of course I can, girl.

POLLY *steps back from Peachum; a brief, embarrassed pause*: Father?

PEACHUM: Yes?

POLLY: I want revenge.

PEACHUM: I absolutely understand, my dear. And how do you propose to get it?

POLLY: Well—I thought—if you have no objection that is—that I might go on seeing him, as though everything was normal between us, but in fact I'd— you know—do what you originally wanted—

PEACHUM: You'd be willing to do that?

POLLY: Perhaps that way I could make amends for what I've done.

PEACHUM: Polly, at last I recognize you for my own daughter. You're magnificent! I knew you wouldn't disappoint me in the end. Look: Macheath was arrested yesterday, but—

POLLY *astonished*: What?

PEACHUM: —but he escaped again last night—

POLLY *excitedly*: Really? How did he manage that?

PEACHUM: They say Lockit's daughter arranged it.

POLLY: Lucy?

PEACHUM: So now he'll be looking for some place to hide—if he hasn't already run off with Lucy. Suppose you were to offer him a place—for the sake of appearances of course? That would strengthen his trust in you and then it would be no problem at all to pry information about his mates out of him, mainly about where the gang has hidden their loot. That wouldn't be a bad little revenge now, would it?

POLLY: Father—

PEACHUM: Yes?

POLLY: Do you really think that Lucy and Macheath could have run off together?

PEACHUM: It wouldn't surprise me in the least!

Polly looks taken aback for a moment, then she whirls around and runs off through the upstage door. Peachum looks after her, surprised.

MRS. PEACHUM: I say—Willy—

PEACHUM: What is it?

MRS. PEACHUM: Do you believe her?

PEACHUM: Of course I do. Why?

MRS. PEACHUM: Don't forget that Macheath has a way with girls.

PEACHUM: Polly wouldn't fall for his tricks, not any more.

MRS. PEACHUM: I only hope she hasn't fallen for them already.

A knock on the right door. Peachum quickly slams his book shut and hides it in the drawer.

PEACHUM *calls out*: Come in!

Ingrid enters.

INGRID: Mr. Peachum?

PEACHUM: What can I do for you?

INGRID: My name is Ingrid.

PEACHUM: I've never heard of you.

INGRID: Madam Diana sent me.

PEACHUM: Ah, so it's you! Splendid. We were expecting you. Come in, sit down and make yourself at home. I'll make some coffee right away.

Scene Ten

Diana's salon again as in scene 8. An angry Betty, standing on the stairs in her underwear, flings a pair of trousers at Jim, who is running down the stairs in long underwear. Jim grabs his trousers in confusion and flees through the right door. At the same time Vicki, with a book in her hand, and Diana come quickly through the upstage right door, drawn by the noise.

DIANA: What's wrong, Betty?

BETTY: He kissed me on the forehead and then had the gall to stroke my hair!

DIANA: What's wrong with that?

BETTY: Madam! I sell my body here as an honest woman, and no cheap bum is going to think he owns my soul as well. What does he think I am?

DIANA: According to your contract, you're obliged to comply with our customers' fantasies.

BETTY: But this wasn't a real honest-to-goodness perversion, it was just pure filth!

VICKI: Betty's right, Madam. We can't let them get away with anything they want. Soon they'd be making declarations of love right to our faces—

BETTY: And we'd end up having to reciprocate!

Betty whirls indignantly and goes back upstairs. At that moment, a breathless Jenny enters through the right door.

DIANA *to Jenny*: Don't tell me you were seeing him out? *Jenny nods awkwardly.* Well, at least he's gone. What did he want?

JENNY: Nothing—he just brought me some messages from Father. They were in the same cell.

VOICE *off*: What's keeping you, Pussycat? Are you coming?

JENNY *toward the left door*: Coming, Your Excellency!

The right door flies open and the sergeant and three bailiffs rush into the room.

SERGEANT: Where is he?

JENNY *pointing to the left upstage door*: In there!

The sergeant and the three bailiffs run across the room and break in through the upstage left door

DIANA: What in God's name is this supposed to mean?

SERGEANT *off*: In the name of His Majesty the King, you are under arrest, sir. From now on, anything you say may be used against you.

JENNY *shouts*: Oh! *She collapses on the stairs; then the sergeant enters through the upstage left door, followed by the bailiffs leading Macheath. At the same time, Betty—now fully dressed—appears on the stairs.*

DIANA: My God, it's Macheath! I had no idea he was here, sergeant—word of honor!

MACHEATH *to Jenny*: Shame on you, you bitch!

The sergeant, followed by the bailiffs and Macheath, exits through the right door. Jenny is sitting on the stairs, staring absently in front of her. A short, embarrassed pause.

DIANA *to Jenny*: What possessed you to hide him here? Don't you know the consequences?

VICKI: That's it, give her a tongue-lashing on top of it all!

VOICE *off*: Pussycat! Pussycat!

BETTY: Vicki's right, Madam. She's head over heels.

DIANA: So much the worse! *To Jenny*: Go back to work! We'll sort this out later.

BETTY: Can't someone else stand in for her? The poor girl's a wreck!

DIANA: All right—Vicki, you're on!

Betty helps Jenny to her feet and leads her off up the stairs; she comes back, sits down in her chair, and resumes knitting the sock. Meanwhile, Vicki walks slowly toward the left door.

VOICE *off*: Pussycat! Pussycat! Please, I beg you, come right away! Come, before it's too—

DIANA *Sitting down behind her desk, shouts irritably toward the left door*: She's on her way.

VOICE *off, with a deep groan of exhaustion*: Ahhhhh! . . . never mind. It's too late—

Vicki mechanically goes back to her place, takes her book and begins reading intently. At the same time, someone knocks at the right door.

DIANA: Come in!

Jack enters. He is wearing a good suit with a boutonniere in his lapel.

JACK: Hello.

DIANA *with a professional smile*: Hello, sir. May I help you?

JACK: I'd like . . .

DIANA: This is your first visit, isn't it?

JACK: Yeah.

DIANA: Please take a seat. *Jack sits down on the taboret.* My salon is not large— there are certainly larger establishments in London—but I have deliberately chosen not to expand. I believe that a service of this kind cannot be provided as though it were some kind of assembly-line product, and those large, anonymous establishments that mechanize and dehumanize the whole business, reducing it to the level of mere consumption, simply go against my grain. I'm sure you'll agree that nothing . . .

Scene Eleven

The prison cell. Everything as in scene 6. Macheath is lying on the cot, his hands in irons. A key rattles in the lock and Macheath quickly gets to his feet. John enters the cell.

JOHN: You've got visitors, Captain.
MACHEATH: I do?
   Polly and Lucy enter the cell. John exits, slamming the door.
   Polly! Lucy!
   Polly steps up to Macheath and slaps him on the cheek.
   What was that for?
   Lucy slaps Macheath's other cheek.
   My God, what's got into you two?
LUCY: You don't know?
POLLY: Everyone told us you were a fraud, a cynic, and a womanizer, but we didn't believe them.
LUCY: We believed your intentions were honest.
POLLY: And we decided to become your partners for life and play our role as best we could, standing by you for better or for worse—
LUCY: Even if it meant going against our own fathers.

POLLY: We gave you everything we had: our fidelity, our love—

LUCY: —our bodies—

POLLY: —our honor—

LUCY: And what did you give us in return? You deceived us shamefully.

POLLY: All that talk of love was a filthy lie—

LUCY —because all you really wanted was to use Polly to gain control of Mr. Peachum's organization—

POLLY: —and to use Lucy to gain influence over Mr. Lockit.

LUCY: We're shocked—

POLLY: —and offended to the very depth of our souls!

POLLY AND LUCY: Shame on you!

A longish pause; Macheath paces about the cell deep in thought, then turns gravely to Polly and Lucy.

MACHEATH: Girls! Girls! I respect your anger, and I understand your pain, because I know that seen from the outside, my behavior may indeed have invited the kind of interpretation your agitated minds have placed on it. But precisely because I understand you, and even more because I know my own faults, I must defend myself where I stand wrongly accused, where your anger prevents you from seeing beneath the surface of my actions to the real, human substance that lies beneath them. In the first place, it is not true that I don't love you. I love you both sincerely, and I have never uttered a word to you that did not reflect my true feelings. Often, in fact, I felt more strongly about you than modesty and pride allowed me to admit. So what have I done to you? Was I wrong to have married you? But what else could I have done? After all, I loved you. Today, of course, such things are usually handled differently. Society finds it more acceptable, and men find it more convenient, to marry only one of the women they love, while—out of a dubious respect for his legitimate spouse's feelings—he banishes the other to second-class status as his mistress, as a slightly better class of prostitute whose duties are virtually those of a wife but whose rights are far inferior, since she is compelled to respect the wife's right to disparage her existence, while not enjoying the slightest right to disparage the wife's existence. At the same time, the wife is equally at a disadvantage. For, while the mistress knows of the wife and often—we may assume—talks about her at great length and in great detail with the husband, the wife must remain submerged in a slough of ignorance, and this quite naturally alienates her from her husband, since the husband is not compelled to hide anything from his mistress—as he must from his wife—so they develop a deeper understanding of each other and the final result is that he grows fonder of the mistress. Can you not see how unfair this arrangement is to both women? And was that the path I was supposed to follow? No, girls, to live up to my responsibilities to you in the fullest possible way, I could not follow other men, but had to go my own way, down a path that would allow both of you an equal degree of legitimacy and dignity. That is the truth, and I ask you to judge me on that basis. Tomorrow, in all probability, I shall be hanged and that will end the matter—although somewhat differently than I had imagined. Clearly then, the future is of no concern to us here, but only the past.

Both Polly and Lucy begin to sob.

When I am no longer here, your memories will be all that remain of me. Only one thing will brighten my final hours and assure that I go content to my death, and that is the hope that those memories will not be unpleasant. Therefore I beseech you, try to put yourselves in my place and understand the logic and the morality of my behavior. Try to see that I have behaved— insofar as I could—honorably. And if you cannot find it in your hearts, even now, when the peace of my soul is at stake, to accept what I have done, then at least try to forgive me. This I beg of you in the name of all those beautiful moments we spent together, and all those fabulous plans that we had no time to bring to fruition.

Polly and Lucy begin to wail; they both fling themselves on Macheath, kissing him passionately and weeping hysterically.

Scene Twelve

The prison office again. Everything as in scene 5. Lockit is lounging behind his desk and looking inquisitively at Filch, who is standing, his arms in shackles, opposite him. John is seated upstage.

LOCKIT: Look here, Filch, there's still one thing I don't quite understand: as a thief by persuasion, pardon the expression, you should actually appreciate the clever way Mr. Peachum works for the underworld, while discharging his duties to the police.

FILCH: I've never held that the ends justify the means. On the contrary, my feeling is that problematic means lead to problematic ends, regardless of how noble those ends might have been.

LOCKIT: I can see you're a man of principle. Then tell me, why did you try to cover for Peachum right to the end, if you so despise his practices?

FILCH: Precisely because I am a man of principle. And one of my principles is: never rat on a colleague, no matter what reservations I may have about him.

LOCKIT: Even if that colleague ratted on you, obviously—

FILCH: Yes.

LOCKIT: You're a strange man, Filch. A pity you're a thief and not a policeman. There's a crying need around here for someone of your integrity.

FILCH: As a policeman, I'm afraid I'd have the same quarrel with you as I have with Peachum.

LOCKIT: Why do you say that?

FILCH: For example, I could never condone the kind of methods you used against me today.

LOCKIT: If you're referring to the stoolie I put in your cell, then you should know that it's a trick as old as the institution of prisons itself. If I'd stuck to your gentlemanly principles, I'd never have found out that my faithful Peachum has been so shamefully deceiving me.

FILCH: I'm sorry, but it was a rotten thing to do.

LOCKIT: Look, Filch, let's just forget it. You don't want to work for the police, and obviously you won't stool for me, so what am I going to do with you? I suppose I have no choice but to tell Gloucester I've caught you—then you'll be of some use to me, at least; the duke will be less inclined to denounce me to the king as a good-for-nothing. Unfortunately, however, that means you-know-what.

FILCH: The noose?

LOCKIT: Gloucester will insist on it.

FILCH: I don't want to go on living anyway. I'm not suited to this world.

LOCKIT: On the contrary, I think the world needs more people like you. A pity, but what else can I do? *To John:* Take him away.

John opens the door left and takes Filch through it into the prison. Shortly afterward there is a knock on the upstage door.

Come in!

Peachum enters and walks over to Lockit, smiling. They shake hands.

PEACHUM: I hope you're not feeling too glum about it, Bill. It happens in the best of prisons.

LOCKIT: What are you talking about?

PEACHUM: There's no need to hide anything from me. I'm well aware that our little bird flew the coop last night.

Peachum sits down on a chair, making himself at home. John comes back through the left door, locks it behind him and exits through the upstage door.

LOCKIT: If you mean Macheath, Willy, he's in cell number six.

PEACHUM: You mean he didn't get away?

LOCKIT: He did, but we caught him again.

PEACHUM: Son of a bitch!

LOCKIT: What's the matter, aren't you pleased?

PEACHUM: Why, of course I'm pleased.

LOCKIT: You don't say that with any sort of conviction. Is anything wrong?

PEACHUM: No—it's just that I thought we might use his escape to wrap the whole case up a bit more shrewdly.

LOCKIT: I'm surprised at you, Willy. I seem to recall that only yesterday you thought Macheath's immediate arrest and sentencing was just about the shrewdest thing we could possibly do.

PEACHUM: Yesterday the situation was different.

LOCKIT: How?

PEACHUM: The point was to act fast, to make sure that Polly wouldn't do anything rash.

LOCKIT: And that's not the point today?

PEACHUM: Polly's come to her senses.

LOCKIT: My, my!

PEACHUM: No, I mean it. She's seen through Macheath, understood the folly of her ways, and now she's volunteered to help me execute my original plan.

LOCKIT: You don't say!

PEACHUM: When I heard Macheath had escaped, my first idea was that Polly could give him a place to hide—for the sake of appearances—regain his confidence, and then find out about his accomplices and the whereabouts of the gang's loot. If it worked, you could round up him and his whole gang and have a monster trial, put the fear of God into the entire underworld. As it is now, his men will all go to ground and strengthen various minor organizations, or start operating independently—and we'll be right back where we started. And on top of it all, we'll make a romantic hero of him— a victim of a woman's treachery.

LOCKIT: I'm sorry, Willy, but a bird in the hand—

PEACHUM: I'm surprised at you, Bill. I seem to recall that only yesterday you were talking differently.

LOCKIT: Yesterday the situation was different.

PEACHUM: How?

LOCKIT: It's not important any more. I had to do it, that's all.

PEACHUM: Because of Lucy?

LOCKIT: I had to make sure she wouldn't do anything rash. I found out she's been married to him for more than a year.

PEACHUM: So this Macheath of ours is a bigamist to boot? If Polly knew that, she'd do anything for us. Why didn't you tell me? No sir, when paternal feelings come into our work, there's always trouble.

LOCKIT: *You* hold that against *me*? That's not very fair. And anyway—why are you suddenly so concerned about Macheath's freedom?

PEACHUM: I hope you're not implying that I wanted to help him.

LOCKIT: I know that Macheath isn't all you're interested in.

PEACHUM: What would I be interested in, then?

LOCKIT: Forget I said that, Willy.

PEACHUM: I know very well what you wanted to say, Bill.

LOCKIT: What did I want to say?

PEACHUM: You think I'm only after the gang's assets, don't you?

LOCKIT: I said nothing of the kind.

PEACHUM: But that's what you think.

LOCKIT: Relax, Willy. If I didn't believe you, I wouldn't even be talking to you like this—especially not after what you told that damned Filch of yours this morning.

PEACHUM: So that's what's eating you, Bill. Now I understand. I had no idea you could be so naive.

LOCKIT: Naive?

PEACHUM: For God's sake, I had to tell him something. What should I have told him? Was I supposed to admit that I work for the police and let him in on our whole game?

LOCKIT: No.

PEACHUM: Well, what then?

LOCKIT: You should have denied everything.

PEACHUM: Bill! The man had proof I turned Macheath in. Don't you see? Denying everything would amount to confirming his suspicion. Even if he'd gone straight to jail, he'd still have had a dozen chances to alert the underworld. Did you expect me to run that kind of risk?

LOCKIT: Why didn't you at least tell me the conversation had taken place?

PEACHUM: I didn't think it was important, and I never once thought you'd misunderstand what I was up to.

LOCKIT: Or maybe you were depending on Filch to keep his mouth shut.

PEACHUM: Bill! My whole position is based entirely on your trust. If I lose that, the game's over. In my situation, the slightest suspicion means an automatic death sentence, and there's no court of appeal.

LOCKIT: You're exaggerating, Willy—

PEACHUM: I'm not exaggerating. Just try putting yourself in my position—it's not asking a lot—and all your doubts will vanish into thin air. *He walks agitatedly around the room, then suddenly turns to face Lockit.* Bill! Have you any idea at all what it's like spending years fighting against the underworld while you're living in it and trying to maintain its confidence? Years of turning evidence against robbers and cutthroats while having to play the role of their benefactor, without a slipup, I might add? Years fighting crime while appearing to commit it? Do you have the slightest inkling of what that means? Wearing two faces for so long? The ceaseless vigilance, day and night, the deception, keeping secrets, pretending to be someone else? Constantly trying to fit into a world you condemn, and to renounce the world to which you really belong? It's so much easier for you: you are what you are; everyone knows what you are, and everyone deals with you accordingly. You don't have to hide anything from anyone, nor pretend, and you needn't adapt. How wonderfully simple your world is! How direct your thoughts can be, how straightforward your points of view: over here is good, right, morality, and over there is evil, wrong, and crime. Unfortunately, what's valid in your world is not valid in mine, and you just can't transfer those values mechanistically from yours to mine without undermining the very foundations on which that world stands. I know that from your perspective, you may often think that I go too far, make senseless compromises, say things I shouldn't, and mimic too closely the world I am struggling to defeat. But it's all so terribly simple for you, sitting here in your cozy little office, out of the wind, making sure your hands are clean, and handing down your simplistic judgments. But try going out into the midst of real life, putting your honor on the line every day of the week by keeping the channels of communication open—for which you will probably never receive proper recognition—and undertaking modest and risky work in the dangerous no-man's-land between the underworld and the police, fighting slowly, inconspicuously on the side of law and order, with no expectation of recognition—that is a very different matter. And anyway, without all that dirty work, so full of sham and undignified compromise, who knows whether this office and this prison would be what they are, a bastion against crime!

LOCKIT: You may be right, Willy. If I've hurt your feelings, please forgive me.

PEACHUM: My feelings are not the point, Bill—

LOCKIT: I know. *A pause.* Say, Willy—

PEACHUM: Yes?

LOCKIT: Do you think, now that Macheath's inside again, that there's really no other way of getting the information we need out of him?

PEACHUM: There is a way, Bill. It's dangerous, but I think it's worth a try.

LOCKIT: What is it?

PEACHUM: Listen carefully.

At that moment, the upstage door flies open and the sergeant enters with the bailiffs, leading the drunk. They walk quickly across the room to the left door; the drunk suddenly stops on the threshold, turns to Lockit, and cries out.

DRUNK: Long live the freedom of the press!

The sergeant slaps the drunk's face.

Scene Thirteen

The prison cell again. Everything as usual. When the scene opens, Macheath is lying—with his hands in shackles—on the cot. A key rattles in the lock and Macheath quickly gets to his feet. John enters.

JOHN: You've got a visitor, Captain.

MACHEATH: I do?

Jenny enters the cell; John exits, slamming the door; Macheath looks at Jenny in astonishment.

JENNY: Surprise.

MACHEATH: I thought you'd come, but I have no time now to waste on things that aren't directly related to my preparations for death. I think it would be best if you left.

JENNY: I won't keep you long. I have to explain everything to you.

MACHEATH: What is there to explain? That you work for the police? That you'll do anything they ask you to? I know that already.

JENNY: You don't know anything.

MACHEATH: What do you mean?

A key rattles in the lock; John enters and addresses Jenny.

JOHN: I'm afraid you'll have to leave, Miss.

JENNY: But I've got a right to half an hour! *Jenny pulls out a piece of paper and shows it to John.* Here's my pass.

JOHN: Mr. Macheath has an important visitor.

JENNY: This is important too.

John whispers something to Macheath, who registers surprise.

JOHN: Leave the cell at once, please!

JENNY *sticking the paper into her bosom:* Very well. I'll wait outside.

John leads Jenny out of the cell. The door remains ajar for a few moments, and then Peachum enters. John slams the door behind him from outside.

PEACHUM: How do you do, Captain.

MACHEATH: I'm honored.

Peachum walks slowly over to the table and sits down; Macheath glowers at him; an awkward pause.

Well, are you satisfied?

PEACHUM: Not in the least. That's why I'm here.

MACHEATH: Why not?

PEACHUM: I went too far. I let myself get carried away in a fit of paternal indignation.

MACHEATH: Maybe you were just angry that your plan to use Polly against me didn't work.

PEACHUM: There's that too.

MACHEATH: At least I'll die happy, knowing you'll have to live with a bad conscience.

PEACHUM: I don't want you to die.

MACHEATH: My, my—and are your pangs of conscience so acute that you're willing to do something about it?

PEACHUM: They are.

MACHEATH: With strings attached, of course.

PEACHUM: Of course.

MACHEATH: That's good, otherwise I wouldn't have believed you. But to get right to the point: I suppose you want my organization's assets.

PEACHUM: I want more than that.

MACHEATH: I don't have more than that.

PEACHUM: Oh, but you do.

MACHEATH: What?

PEACHUM: You have capable people, a visionary business plan, a wealth of experience, good ideas—

MACHEATH: Isn't that asking a little too much?

PEACHUM: Isn't life worth it? This is a serious offer.

MACHEATH: I'm listening.

PEACHUM: I'm offering you a merger.

MACHEATH: A merger?

PEACHUM: Restructuring, to be more precise. Your organization would merge with mine completely. You would be my vice-president, with all the corresponding privileges and duties. And if I die before you do, you take over the whole business.

MACHEATH: That's it?

PEACHUM: There's another condition: you must lead a proper married life with Polly. She's very fond of you; I found that much out today, when she promised to help me destroy you. She's not in the habit of lying to me, but she did this time, and it could only have been dictated by an extraordinary love for you.

MACHEATH: You've obviously realized that it's better for you to have me working for you alive than against you dead. Isn't that it?

PEACHUM: Yes. And at the same time, I assumed that you'd probably prefer being alive as a decent husband and deputy head of the organization to being a dead boss and a notorious dead ladies' man.

MACHEATH: It's easier to get someone into jail than out of it. How would you persuade Lockit to let me go?

PEACHUM: You must know I have ways of influencing him.

MACHEATH: I had thought it was he who had ways of influencing you.

PEACHUM: What's that supposed to mean?

MACHEATH: Look, my friend, let's stop playing games. You must think I'm a bigger fool than I am.

PEACHUM: I don't know what you mean.

MACHEATH: Did you seriously think I'd swallow all this?

PEACHUM: So you think there's a hidden trick? Now where would that get me? I stand to do well by the proposal as it is.

MACHEATH: You would stand to do well if you'd concentrate on developing your own enterprise, not on cooperating with the police. But since that's not the case, I see your offer as no more than a clever maneuver you and Lockit have worked out so you can seize my assets, arrest all my men, and hold a monster trial. But if I'm going to hang, I'd rather hang as a hero who stood by his comrades, condemned alongside them for robbery—a tragic victim of feminine wiles—than as a traitor to his mates.

PEACHUM: My friend, I had no idea I'd have to spell it all out for you—here, of all places. But I see you're more naive than I thought.

MACHEATH: I understand only too well, my friend.

Peachum looks around, then moves closer to Macheath and speaks in lowered tones.

PEACHUM: You don't understand a thing, you fool! Of course the whole idea started in Lockit's office. But how else could I have done it? You think Lockit would let someone out of here just on my say-so? I swear I don't have that kind of influence with him. So I invented this plan to offer you a merger and get you out of here. Lockit would be on the trail and he'd be able to round you up with your gang. But why do you think I did it? For the same reason I always have: to fill Lockit's glass with Peachum's wine, that's why. Why do you think I cooperate with the police? Because I love the king? I'm just doing what everyone else is doing—in one way or another: working for my own ends and covering my back at the same time.

MACHEATH: So, you want to put one over on Lockit?

PEACHUM: What else?

MACHEATH: What's to prevent him from carrying out the second part of the plan and grabbing me and my boys after the merger?

PEACHUM: Don't you suppose, my friend, that in all the years I've been playing these games with him, I haven't learned something? I could tell him the underworld knows about our plan and that if he went through with it, it would blow my cover.

MACHEATH: Hmm. And how do I know this isn't just another scheme you've concocted with Lockit?

PEACHUM: It's a matter of trust, my friend. After all, I have no way of know-ing you won't betray me either. You'll simply have to decide whether to risk it or not. As far as I'm concerned, I've already made up my mind.

MACHEATH: All right. I accept.

PEACHUM: Wonderful. I'll expect you tomorrow evening in my house. I hope this is the beginning of an era of constructive cooperation for both of us. Farewell, Captain.

MACHEATH: Good-bye.

Peachum exits. Macheath paces around the cell, thinking. Then a key rattles in the lock and John enters.

JOHN: Can I bring the lady back?

MACHEATH: Is she still here?

JOHN *calls off:* Miss!

Jenny enters the cell; John exits, slamming the door.

MACHEATH: So, you want me to believe you're not working for the police?

JENNY: I want to tell you the truth.

MACHEATH: You've told me that already—at Diana's.

JENNY: That was different.

MACHEATH: Oh? How is that?

JENNY: If I hadn't tried to persuade you I was telling the truth, that little com-edy about my condemned father wouldn't have made any sense.

MACHEATH: And they wouldn't have caught me, would they?

JENNY: That's exactly it! So far, I've lied to you only to get you into prison. Why should I lie to you now that you're here?

MACHEATH: Fine. And what's the truth for today?

JENNY: I'm not working for Lockit.

MACHEATH: Aha! First they forced you to betray me in the tavern and then they forced you to betray me at Diana's by admitting that you'd betrayed me in the tavern only under duress. Very cleverly worked out, but this time I'm not falling for it.

JENNY: That's not what I'm trying to claim.

MACHEATH: Wonderful—so you admit that you're working for them.

JENNY: Nothing is the way you think it is.

MACHEATH: Tell me about it.

JENNY: It's worse!

MACHEATH: Worse! What could be any worse than that?

JENNY: Look, if I had betrayed you twice in a row—as you assume—simply because it was part of my job, or to get in good with the police, it would still be understandable. But I had no such reasons.

MACHEATH: Are you trying to say that no one put you up to it, or that there was nothing in it for you?

JENNY: The first time, I volunteered my services, and as a matter of fact, it took a lot of persuasion before they would agree to it. The second time I did it entirely on my own.

MACHEATH: Something like evil for evil's sake?

JENNY: Yes.

MACHEATH: And I'm supposed to believe that?

JENNY: Why would I make something like that up?

MACHEATH: Because maybe Lockit ordered you to take the blame. That's obviously the real reason behind this visit too.

JENNY: Do you think Mr. Lockit needs to look good to someone who's in no position to cause him any more trouble?

MACHEATH: All right. You're claiming that twice in a row, you betrayed me out of pure inner compulsion?

JENNY: Perverse, isn't it?

MACHEATH: That depends. From a certain point of view, it would be more attractive than betraying me for money. For one thing it wouldn't be nearly as banal.

JENNY: But that's not all. I needed to destroy you so badly that when they took you away, I didn't even feel guilty about it, as people usually do in such cases. On the contrary, I was overwhelmed by a strange sensation of physical pleasure. Do you still find it more attractive than other forms of betrayal?

MACHEATH: You may be surprised, but if it were true, I think I'd rather like the idea. At least there'd be some passion in it, and I always respect passion.

JENNY: There's no need to be so gallant; I'd be satisfied if you'd believe me.

MACHEATH: You have no idea how happy I'd be to believe that I could believe you.

JENNY: But just because I didn't feel guilty it doesn't mean that I have never felt guilt, or don't feel it now. On the contrary: I've thought a lot about my strange behavior, and I've asked myself where it came from so suddenly—because until then I'd never done anything like it.

MACHEATH: Well, at least I was your first in something.

JENNY: Don't be cruel.

MACHEATH: And where did those thoughts lead you?

JENNY: Look, Mack—you can't exist as two different people—one who does the will of others, and the other who looks on in disgust. We all need—to a certain extent, anyway—to belong to ourselves, because not belonging to ourselves means not having an identity, and therefore, de facto, not to *be* at all. As you know, my profession compels me to belong to myself less than other women. The thing they often consider their most valuable asset, doesn't, in my case, belong to me at all, but to the marketplace. Yet I want to belong to myself because I want to *be* myself. Is it any wonder that I am all the more protective of the little of me that is still under my control, and thanks to which I still *am* at all?

MACHEATH: I assume you mean your heart?

JENNY: Maybe it's an occupational hazard; the less our bodies belong to us, the more energetic we are in defending the independence of our hearts. I don't know if you can understand that, but I feel a tremendous need to resist anyone who threatens to subdue my heart.

MACHEATH: But surely that doesn't apply to me.

JENNY: It does, Mack—

MACHEATH: You love me?

JENNY: I'd never admit it if I didn't know you were going to die.

MACHEATH: And how on earth did that happen? You hardly know me.

JENNY: I don't know. I saw you a couple of times at the salon, and I've heard people talk about you a little. For a long time I wasn't even aware of it, but the longer that fire smoldered away in my subconscious, the more violent the flames that ravaged my consciousness. I was beside myself; I walked about in a daze, hating you and cursing you; my pride became helpless anger—and then it happened: I realized that if I ever wanted to belong to myself again, I had to destroy you. Yes, my humiliation could only be wiped out by bloody vengeance, in a drastic act of self-affirmation. I had to kill you in order to live.

MACHEATH: Jenny, don't you realize that you become yourself only through your relationships to others—and primarily through love? If you suppress that love, you are suppressing what is most yourself, the very thing that could make you truly what your are. What has made you lose yourself is not love, but pride; you have let your pride enslave you—that destructive affect of the mind that drives you into the strange vacuum of loneliness where you have nothing to compare yourself to and, therefore, no identity. Jenny, please understand this: I am not entering your heart to destroy its sovereignty, but as a living incarnation of its own sovereign will. I would not lead you away from yourself, but on the contrary, I'm the only possible mediator of your return to selfhood; I am not taking your existence away from you, but making it more profound. I am not your ruin, but your salvation.

JENNY: It's easy for you to talk; you're not like me at all. And anyway, it doesn't work if only one of us is in love.

MACHEATH: Jenny, don't be foolish! Why do you think that I—who have never before been betrayed by any woman—allowed myself so easily to be deceived by you, not once, but twice? True, I wasn't aware of it at first, but now it's obvious: I'd never have let myself become ensnared if you hadn't managed to charm me with that special, passionate and darkly dramatic nature of yours, of which you have just now given me a glimpse. Yes, now I know at last what it was about you that excited me so profoundly that I cast aside my usual caution: it was your pride, your dark compulsion to commit evil, your haughtiness and the searing sensuality that lurks behind it. Jenny, it makes no sense to deny it to myself or to you any longer: I love you too! I love you despite the fact that you betrayed me, and in a very strange way, I love you precisely because you betrayed me. Believe me, I had no idea betrayal could be so erotic.

JENNY: You see? You offer me a life of harmony and love, and on the other hand you admit that all you love about me is the fact that I've betrayed you. Mack, the two of us could never be happy together; whether I destroy you or not, I will always kill our love—it's simply a vicious circle.

MACHEATH: Jenny, your betrayal excited me because it overpowered your love; how much more exciting will your love be when it overpowers your need to betray!

JENNY: You're a dreadful man, Mack! I was certain of my victory and now I see that if I don't betray you immediately, it will be the end of me.

MACHEATH: On the contrary, this moment is a new beginning for us. Today, they're letting me go, and the two of us will flee together, somewhere far away where no one will ever find us, save for the birds and the stars.

Scene Fourteen

The Lockit household. Except for a few highly visible but superficial differences—the color scheme, for example—it is the same as the interior of the Peachums' house. When the scene opens, Lockit and Mrs. Lockit are onstage. Lockit, in a housecoat, is sitting at the table writing in a large ledger; Mrs. Lockit, in an apron, is busy around the stove, cooking supper. A long pause, then Mrs. Lockit speaks.

MRS. LOCKIT: Bill . . .

LOCKIT *without looking up*: What is it?

MRS. LOCKIT: D'you think it was a good idea?

LOCKIT: Do I think *what* was a good idea?

MRS. LOCKIT: Sorting out that business with Macheath so radically.

LOCKIT: It was the only thing we could have done, Mary.

A knock on the right door. Lockit quickly slams the ledger shut and hides it in the desk drawer.

Come in!

HAROLD *enters through the right door*: Boss, I'd like to report that the execution order on Filch has just been carried out.

LOCKIT: How did he behave?

HAROLD: Bravely, sir. Just before he dropped, he called out: "Long live the London underworld."

LOCKIT: A happy man. He remained true to himself even unto death. *Harold is about to leave.* Harold—

HAROLD: Yes, boss?

LOCKIT: Does Macheath have any visitors at the moment?

HAROLD: Don't think so.

LOCKIT: Then bring him here, please.

Harold exits right; Lockit takes his book out of the drawer and begins writing something in it.

MRS. LOCKIT: Bill . . .

LOCKIT *without looking up*: What is it?

MRS. LOCKIT: Why do you want to see Macheath?

LOCKIT: You'll see.

MRS. LOCKIT: Are you going to give him another chance?

LOCKIT: Why should I do that?

MRS. LOCKIT: I'm afraid Lucy might do something rash.

LOCKIT: Oh, come my dear—

A knock on the right door. Lockit quickly slams his book shut and hides it in the drawer.

Come in!

Harold enters leading Macheath, whose hands are shackled.

HAROLD: Here he is, boss.

LOCKIT: Could you wait in the hall, just in case? *Harold exits though the right door; Lockit stares at Macheath intensely for a moment, then points to a chair.* Have a seat.

MACHEATH: Thanks.

Macheath sits down at the table opposite Lockit and looks at him curiously.

LOCKIT: Yesterday you cursed me for locking you up at Peachum's request— do you remember?

MACHEATH: Indeed—

LOCKIT: And now you believe that at the request of this very same Peachum, I want to let you go, is that right?

MACHEATH *taken aback*: Why, no—

LOCKIT: No? What was Peachum doing in your cell today?

MACHEATH: He came to make his peace with me.

LOCKIT: Didn't he also happen to say that he could get you out of here if you'd agree to merge your two organizations?

MACHEATH: No—

LOCKIT: Oh, yes he did. He and I had it all worked out; it was a trick designed to get you to reveal the whereabouts of your people before we finally hanged you.

MACHEATH: Why are you telling me this?

LOCKIT: It doesn't make any difference now.

MACHEATH: Why not?

LOCKIT: Because unfortunately you didn't fall for it. Peachum tried to save the situation by claiming that he had only pretended to work out the plan with me—just to get you out—and that was merely a backup plan in case you didn't believe the first one, and you didn't even fall for that—

MACHEATH: What do you mean? I accepted Peachum's offer!

LOCKIT: Yes, but only so you could get out, take control—through a counterfeit merger of the assets of both organizations—and then, before I could run you and your boys to ground, you would have run off with a certain lady to a place where no one would find you—save for the birds and the stars. *Macheath jumps up.* In other words, when you understood that Peachum was double-crossing you when he said he was double-crossing me, you decided to double-cross him. But—luckily for us and unluckily for you—you yourself were double-crossed shortly thereafter. Now do you understand?

MACHEATH *aghast and speechless for a moment, then*: That bitch! *He sinks back into his chair, staring ahead of him, crushed; Lockit and his wife exchange meaningful smiles.* Then it's all over.

LOCKIT: You always have a second chance, Mackie. In this prison, anyway.

MACHEATH: I don't want to go on living. I'm not suited to this world.

LOCKIT: I wish you wouldn't overdramatize.

A long pause.

MACHEATH: All right. What are you waiting for? My neck is at your disposal!

LOCKIT: I'm waiting for you to calm down. *To Mrs. Lockit:* Mary, I think a spot of brandy for the Captain?

Mrs. Lockit pours some brandy into a glass and sets it in front of Macheath.

MRS. LOCKIT: There you are.

MACHEATH: Thank you . . .

A pause. Macheath stares gloomily at the floor, mechanically sipping his drink; Lockit watches him intently. Finally, Macheath speaks in a subdued voice.
Well, what's the deal?

LOCKIT: Look here, Mackie. Peachum, as you've already gathered, is working for me and enjoys my full confidence. But precisely because he is so reliable, his service deserves to be based on something more solid than mere trust. I need evidence.

MACHEATH: What do you want me to do?

LOCKIT: Nothing more and nothing less than to go through with this merger Peachum is offering you, and then all you have to do—as his VP—is to keep your eyes open and tell me what's new in the business from time to time, how your new boss is doing and whether he is in fact turning all his profits over to the city treasury. That's all. If you agree, I'll guarantee your security and the security of your boys. What do you say?

MACHEATH: You're not afraid I'll double-cross you?

LOCKIT: How?

MACHEATH: What if I discover that Peachum is cheating you, but I cover up for him, or even band together with him against you?

LOCKIT: You won't.

MACHEATH: How do you know?

LOCKIT: In the first place, you'll never be sure whether any evidence of Peachum's betrayal isn't just something I set in motion to test your reliability—and you may rest assured I will plant such evidence from time to time. In the second place, Peachum will inform me at once of any attempt on your part to work out a deal behind my back. If he is loyal to me, he will do it out of zeal; and if not, he'll report it anyway for fear it's a test of his loyalty set in motion by me—and you may rest assured I will plant such evidence from time to time. So how about it? Do you accept?

A long, tense pause; Macheath paces up and down the room thinking hard, then suddenly he turns to Lockit.

MACHEATH: Look here, Lockit: I don't cling to my life; I'm not afraid of death, and I'm even willing to die—of course, only on condition that in doing so I will reinforce the values I am dying for, and that through my death I will improve the lot of others. I did not give myself life and it does not belong to me—I am merely its steward—and what kind of steward would I be if I were to pointlessly destroy what I have been given to safeguard? If, as it's turned out, everyone around me has double-crossed me, this does not mean that they expect me to be any different, but just the opposite: by deceiving me, they are in fact offering me a principle on which to base our mutual relations. If I were to turn that offer down, those around me would understand it as an ostentatious expression of my own superiority and conceit—all the more so because it would be followed by that theatrical coda—my execution—and everyone would ask: where does he get the right to be so different from the rest of us, to step out of line, to thumb his nose at the opinions of the majority and to spit on that minimum of discipline without which no society can function properly? I would be seen as a pompous and arrogant exhibitionist, someone who wanted to play the conscience of the world. I'd be giving my life for something no one but me believes in. My death would therefore remain uncomprehended; it would reinforce no values, it would help no one, and merely cause pain to those closest to me. It would, in short, be a typically meaningless death. And I can understand that: to utterly reject the rules of the game this world offers may well be the easier way, but it usually leads nowhere. It is far more difficult, and at the same time far more meaningful, to accept those rules, thus enabling one to communicate with those around one, and then to put that ability to work in the gradual struggle for better rules. In other words, the only truly dignified and manly solution to my dilemma is to turn and face life head on, plunge bravely into its stormy waters, fearing not the filth and the obstacles life places in my way, but investing all my strength and all my skill in the struggle to make life better than it is.

10. A *tableau vivant* onstage at the end of the play.

LOCKIT: Spoken like a true man, Mackie. I'm deeply moved.

   Lockit offers Macheath his hand. They both shake, rather awkwardly, since
   Macheath's hands are shackled. Then Lockit takes a piece of paper, a pen and an
   inkwell from his drawer and places them ceremoniously in front of Macheath.

   Now, if you'll just sign here—

MACHEATH: Wouldn't my word be enough?

LOCKIT: No.

   Macheath sits down at the table and with great difficulty signs the document;
   Lockit watches him closely. As soon as it is signed, he snatches it away, blows on

11. Andrej Krob supervises the tearing down of the set.

it, puts it back in the drawer, and then offers his hand to Macheath again; the complications, of course, are repeated.
I hope this is the beginning of an era of sound and constructive cooperation for both of us. *Calls toward right door.* Harold! *Harold enters.* Take them off. *Harold removes the shackles from Macheath, who shakes his arms gently to relax his stiffened muscles.*
You're a free man, Mackie. God speed!

MACHEATH *Still shaking his arms, he bows to Mrs. Lockit, who is setting the table for supper.* Madam, I take my leave.

MRS. LOCKIT *smiling:* I hope, now that everything has turned out so well, that you'll leave your profligate ways and live with Lucy. She's so fond of you!

MACHEATH: You can count on me, mother! *To Lockit:* Ciao!

Macheath exits through the right door, followed by Harold. Mrs. Lockit serves the soup and then sits down to supper with Lockit.

LOCKIT *tucking a serviette into his collar:* Well, Mary, from this moment on our organization has practically the entire underworld of London under its control.

MRS. LOCKIT: It took a bit of doing, didn't it?

LOCKIT: Gaining control of the London Police Force was a piece of cake by comparison.

MRS. LOCKIT: It's still bizarre though, Bill. No one knows about our organization, yet everyone works for it.

LOCKIT: They serve best who know not that they serve. Bon appétit!

Lockit and Mrs. Lockit begin eating.